DATE DUE

MY 26 93			

DEMCO 38-296

THE INDIVIDUAL
IN THE
ANIMAL KINGDOM

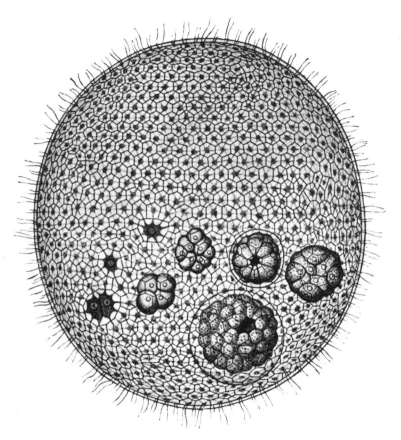

Volvox globator Ehrenberg. An adult asexual colony, highly magnified. The hexagonal areas represent the gelatinous coats of the individual cells in surface view. The thin common envelope of the whole colony is seen round the circumference. In the hinder half of the colony are seen two of the large asexual reproductive cells, and various stages of their development into daughter-colonies. The two most advanced daughter-colonies have already secreted a common envelope of their own. (After A. Lang.)

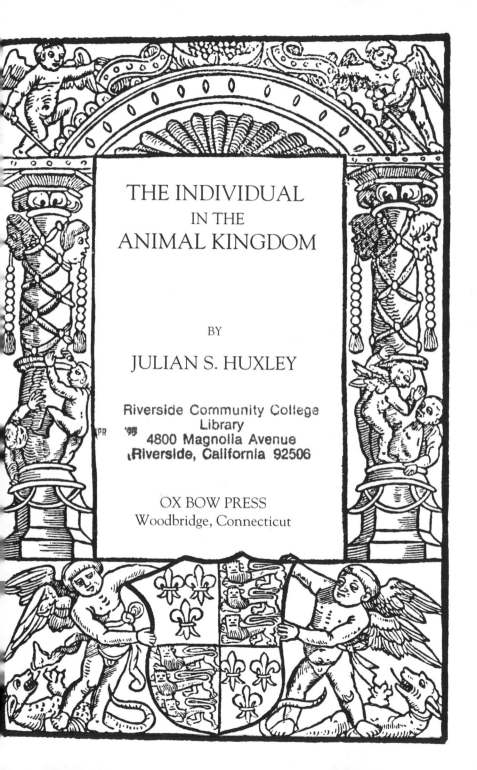

THE INDIVIDUAL
IN THE
ANIMAL KINGDOM

BY

JULIAN S. HUXLEY

OX BOW PRESS
Woodbridge, Connecticut

1995 Reprint published by:
OX BOW PRESS
P.O. Box 4045
Woodbridge, Connecticut, U.S.A. 06525
(203) 387-5900   FAX (203) 387-0035

Library of Congress Cataloging-in-Publication Data

Huxley, Julian, 1887-1975.
        The individual in the animal kingdom / by Julian S.
Huxley.
                p.   cm.
        Originally published: Cambridge, Eng. : University Press;
    New York : G.P. Putnam's Sons, 1912, in series: The
    Cambridge manuals of science and literature.
        Includes bibliographical references (p.   ) and index.
    ISBN 1-881987-05-1 (cloth : alk. paper)
        1. Life (Biology) -- Philosophy.   2. Individuality.
        I.Title.
QH501.H88   1994
113'.8 -- dc20   94-9409
                                                                          CIP

The design on the cover and title page is a reproduction
of one used by the earliest known Cambridge printer,
John Siberch, 1521.

The paper in this book meets the guidelines for performance and durability of the
Committee on Production Guidelines for Book Longevity of the Council on
Library Resources.

Printed in the United States of America

PREFACE

I MUST confess that when I made choice of Animal Individuality as my subject, I had no idea of its real importance, its vastness and many ramifications: the teaching of philosophical biology is in England to-day somewhat of a Cinderella. The working out of the concept, full of interest as it was, brought also regret; a book of the size could have been—should have been—made from every twig and a stout octavo from the central trunk. This might not be; and the unavoidable compression must be pardoned. The general reader must imitate the Organic Individual (p. 26) and take unto himself wings of thought and conscious effort to skip across the unbridged gaps that perforce remain; with them to aid, I think he will find the stepping-stones not too far apart. The professed biologist must not cavil when he finds some merely general truth set dogmatically down as universal; in biology (still so empirical and tentative) there are always exceptions to the poor partial "Laws" we can formulate to-day. To have qualified every statement that needed qualification would have added much to the book's bulk without aiding the argument or being really more "scientific."

My indebtednesses are great. It will easily be seen how much I owe to M. Bergson, who, whether one agrees or no with his views, has given a stimulus (most valuable gift of all) to Biology and Philosophy

alike. The various Oxford philosopher-friends who
have helped to comb out the tangles of a zoologist's
mind know how grateful I am to them: I will not
name them here for fear my heresies be laid to their
charge.

Certain criticisms have convinced me that some
explanation of the scope of this book will here not
be out of place. The task I have attempted in the
following pages is a two-fold one. First, I have tried
to frame a general definition of the Individual,
sufficiently objective to permit of its application by
the man of science, while at the same time admitted
as accurate (though perhaps regarded as incomplete)
by the philosopher. Secondly, I have tried to show
in what ways Individuality, *as thus defined by me*,
manifests itself in the Animal Kingdom.

I wish here to point out in general, that the
failure of one of these aims does *not* preclude the
success of the other ; and, in particular, this :—it is
possible that the philosophically-minded will quarrel
with my definition of the Individual (p. 28) as a
"continuing whole with inter-dependent parts" (to
put it at its baldest). But even if he denies that
the definition applies to the Individual, he must, I
think, admit that it does apply to something, and to
something which plays a very important part in the
organic world. He will, I believe, after reading the
subsequent chapters, be brought to see that every
living thing is in some way related to one of these

systems, these continuing wholes; and that such wholes, though they may not in his eyes deserve the name of Individual, are yet sufficiently widespread and important to merit some title of their own. Put in other words, the major portion of this book is devoted to showing that living matter always tends to group itself into these "closed, independent systems with harmonious parts." Though the closure is never complete, the independence never absolute, the harmony never perfect, yet systems and tendency alike have real existence. Such systems I personally believe can be identified with the Individuals treated of by the philosopher, and I have tried to establish this belief. But what's in a name? *the systems are there whatever we may choose to call them,* and if I have shown that, I shall be content.

In conclusion, I will only hope that this little book may help, however slightly, to decrease still further the gap (to-day happily lessening) between Science, Philosophy, and the ideas and interests of everyday life.

J. S. HUXLEY.

BALLIOL COLLEGE,
OXFORD.
Sept., 1912.

The numbers in brackets to be found in the text refer to the Bibliography at the end of the book.

An Appendix has also been added, giving some of the main conclusions in tabular form.

CONTENTS

LIST OF ILLUSTRATIONS

Figs. 2, 10, and 11 are reproduced from the *Encyclopaedia Britannica* (eleventh edition); figs. 6 and 12 are from Lankester's *Treatise on Zoology*, Vol. II, and Scott's *Structural Botany* respectively, by kind permission of Messrs A. & C. Black; fig. 7 is from West's *British Freshwater Algae* (Camb. Univ. Press); and fig. 13 is from Weismann's *Evolution Theory*, by permission of Mr Edward Arnold.

THE INDIVIDUAL
IN THE
ANIMAL KINGDOM

CHAPTER I

THE IDEA OF INDIVIDUALITY

"Die Zeit ist abgeflossen, wo mir noch Zufälle begegnen durften; und was *könnte* jetzt noch zu mir fallen, was nicht schon mein Eigen wäre!"   NIETZSCHE.

"La vie manifeste une recherche de l'individualité et tend à constituer des systèmes naturellement isolés, naturellement clos."
                                                                                        BERGSON.

"ACCIDENTS cannot happen to me." So says Nietzsche's Zarathustra, and in the saying proclaims to the world the perfection of his individuality. It might be thought that such a being was far outside the purview of the Zoologist, that he himself belonged to imagination and his individuality to the most speculative philosophy, and that both he and it should be left where they belong, where they could not contaminate the "pure objective truth of science."

That I think is an error: for the idea of individuality is dealt with of necessity both by Science and by Philosophy, and in such a difficult subject it would be mistaken to reject any sources of help. Not only that, but animal individuality with the advent of consciousness, though still remaining a lawful subject of the Zoologist, becomes naturalised in the proper realms of the Psychologist and the Philosopher and transfers thither the major portion of its business.

More, even were the Zoologist to confine himself to a description of non-conscious organic individuals and the deductions he drew from them, he would often find himself without a reasoned criterion of Individuality or a true idea of what he means by "higher" or "lower" individualities. It is only when the Biologist and the Philosopher join hands that they can begin to see the subject in its entirety.

There are two chief ways of enquiry into the meaning of things—the static and the dynamic. In determining the nature of Individuality, for instance, we may seek to define it by comparing the different objects we are agreed upon to call individuals and then taking their Highest Common Measure—extracting from them the utmost which is common to all and erecting that as the minimum conception of Individuality ; or we may search for the movement of individuality through the individuals, and, finding that some are more perfect, some more rudimentary in their individuality, thus establish a direction in which its movement is tending, and from that deduce the properties of the Perfect Individual, possessing then a maximum conception of Individuality.

In view of the change, the progressive change or
evolution which is one of the fundamental things of
Life, the second method is the more natural, and in
a way includes the first. Using it in the main,
therefore, but not rejecting the other as an engine,
we will begin to lay siege to the notion of individuality; and so, having justified the necessity
for some philosophical view of the subject, but with
apologies none the less for a biologist's intrusion on
another's domain, we return to Zarathustra and his
pronouncement.

"Accidents do not happen to me."—When a glance
is thrown over the various forms of animal life to
which the name of Individual is naturally conceded[1],
it is seen that in spite of many side-ventures, they
can be arranged in a single main series in which
certain characters are manifested more clearly and
more thoroughly at the top than at the bottom. One
of these characters is independence of the outer

---

[1] There may appear to be a vicious circle in the use of the word
individual before we know its definition; in reality there is not.
The word individual has not been manufactured to label a theoretical
concept, but to denote something existing. It was originally applied
to human beings, and a special word had to be used for them because
it was felt that they differed in certain important ways from mere
things. Certain other objects (all of them organic, but together
making only a portion of the whole organic world) are immediately
recognized as possessing similar attributes, and it is obvious that
they too must be Individuals, although equally obvious that we have
only used, without defining, the category "Individual."

world and all its influences—in other words, immunity
from accidents. By independence is not meant the
independence of the recluse or the ascetic, but that
other independence belonging to the great man of
action and the inventor. These are not independent
in the most literal sense—they do not "do without,"
they are not proud of existing on the barest minimum;
the ultimate logical end of that kind of independence
is atrophy, both mental and physical. Their other,
higher independence involves this much of dependence,
that they employ the things of the external world as
material with which to work. For the making of
bricks, you are dependent upon straw: but you
attain a higher independence by making bricks and
being dependent upon straw than by being independent of straw and lacking bricks. They gain
their independence by using the outer world for
their own ends, harnessing some of its forces to
strive with and overcome the rest. At the least
they can resist the adverse current, displaying
a purpose of their own which is not whirled away
by every wind of fate. "Accidents cannot happen
to me"—so spake Zarathustra, and then added this
reason: "Because all that could now happen to me
would be my own."

In this making of Nature his own, civilized man
has an individuality vastly fuller, more perfect, than
the savage. Both in resisting adverse forces and in

harnessing the indifferent to his will, he is far superior; take as a concrete instance, for one the stamping out of malaria in the Suez Canal zone, and for the other the invention of the microscope. At the other end of the series, even the simplest Protozoan has something of the same power. Although in a current against which the savage (let alone the steamboat of the civilised man) could easily swim, the Protozoan is carried utterly away, yet none the less it has some power of independent movement, and is not helpless like the inorganic grain of dust.

This gradual increase of independence up from the Protozoa to the highest animals is due partly to mere increase of size[1] : the same current that carries the grain of sand in its midst and rolls the pebble on its bed, swirls powerless past the boulder.

Partly it is due to increased complexity : the actions of the caterpillar who once in his life weaves an elaborate cradle to support his transmuted pupa-self, without either practice or the sight of another to teach him, can only be due to the actual machinery of his brain, working in a way almost as stereotyped as our machines,—a long series of ready-wound clock-work which must unwind itself when a certain catch is released. The Protozoan or the Jelly-fish is not capable of such precise and ordered action because it

[1] See pp. 85—89 for some further treatment of the value of size.

has not the requisite machinery, the requisite complication of brain and muscle. Lastly it is due to increased adaptability, which depends mainly upon increased power of choice. Adaptability seems to be a property soon acquired by a complex and unstable substance, or rather mixture of substances, like protoplasm. Roux (16) by extending Darwin's idea of Natural Selection or survival of the fittest from individuals to the organs and tissues, the cells and varieties of protoplasm within the individual, has shown that some measure of adaptability, or useful response to changed conditions, becomes a common property of all living things. This, though very important, has been slow in action, merely automatic, and therefore limited in its usefulness, the result, to speak in metaphors, not of choice but of habit. What we call choice has only become fully realized through a special arrangement of special tissue—the brain.

Says Bergson: "A nervous system with neurones placed end to end in such wise that, at the extremity of each, manifold ways open in which manifold questions present themselves, is a veritable reservoir of indetermination" (1, p. 133). Such is the nervous system of man : and whatever value we assign to the idea of indetermination, whether we believe in the reality of choice and free-will, or think that they are only apparent, due to the relativity of our mental powers, the fact remains that in a brain which is constructed after the pattern of our own, and in which therefore we postulate the existence of Consciousness, a new machinery, different in kind from any machinery we have been able to construct, has been introduced; machinery that by supplying the individual with memory and reason gives him the largest scope to adjust his actions, and so himself, to the variations of circumstance.

Civilized man is the most independent, in our sense, of any animal: this he owes partly to his comparatively large size, more to his purely mechanical complexity of body and brain, giving him the possibility of many precise and separate actions, and most to the unique machinery of part of his brain which enables him to use his size and the smoothly-working machine-actions of his body in the most varied way.

But he is far from perfect independence of accidents. A being to whom accidents really could not happen might attain to that happy state through having perfected himself in any of the three qualities which have been seen to assist independence. By incorporating more and more matter—that is, by increasing in size—until co-extensive with the universe, he would obviously be entirely independent; there would remain nothing on which to be dependent. Since matter is what it is, man at least has little

chance of advancing far along that road. By building
up within himself a separate machine for dealing with
each possible eventuality, independence would like-
wise be obtained were it not that there is an infinity of
eventualities, and so the project is self-contradictory.
But by perfecting his mental attributes—his means
of perceiving, remembering, and reasoning—he would
become capable of dealing with any one of the infinite
eventualities, for though he could not construct an
infinity of machines simultaneously, yet as each new
eventuality cropped up, he would be able to invent a
new plan to cope with it. Though Zarathustra had
climbed far up this path, he probably was not quite
accurate about the accidents: it is not likely that he
would be able to experience everything, to remember
everything, and to understand everything, but so alone
would he be altogether immune from the accidental.
That is neither here nor there. The chief importance
lies in this: all life of which we have any assured
cognizance is dependent upon or inseparably associated with a certain kind of matter—protoplasm.
Knowing what we do of the properties of protoplasm,
it becomes evident that no considerable advance
towards independence through either of the first two
methods is physically possible for life ; it is only the
third way, with its multiplication of potentialities,
which, in spite of size really not so hugely great and
mechanism really not so vastly complex, can yet give

life a considerable fresh amount of immunity from accident. The second quotation at the head of this chapter seems at first sight to take a very different view of the individual, conceiving of it as "a system naturally isolated, naturally closed." By this Bergson means that in any consideration of that system, it is the unity of it as a whole that is important: more than that, even if you want to consider a part of the system by itself, you cannot do so, for it loses almost all its significance when detached from the whole. What is the meaning of the hand and its actions apart from the functioning of the whole body? More striking still, for here there are no physical connections to sever, what is the meaning of a lonely bee and its actions when it comes back to find its hive destroyed? With inorganic things on the other hand, a part does not lose significance when detached from a system, nor the system appear less perfect for the detachment of the part. The inorganic system is a Particular, but not an Individual. Cause half a mountain to be removed and cast into the sea: what remains is still a mountain, though a different one. Take away a planet, and the Solar System still works: its working is different, but, as far as we can see, only different, not less perfect.

Nietzsche's words affirmed the individual's principle of action: Bergson's point out the inner unity for the good of which that action is performed. From the latter we can deduce another attribute of individuality—its heterogeneity; from that very unity of the whole we can postulate diversity of its parts. This sounds paradoxical, but in reality it can be easily shown that nothing homogeneous can be an individual.

Suppose (as is highly probable) that the earliest forms of life were homogeneous in chemical composition. If so, even were they compelled by the nature of things (see Chap. II) to exist as separate masses of defined shape and size, even though, by reason of their complicated atomic structure, they could carry on all the diverse functions necessary for their continued existence with their one chemical substance, they would then not be individuals. There is no unity residing in such masses—they are the merest aggregates; whether you divided one into two or twenty or a hundred pieces it would still go on working in the same way, without a break[1], whereas if you divide a man into two by cutting off his hand, the working of the main part—the man—is rendered less effective, and that of the lesser part—the hand—

[1] That is, of course, supposing the external world and the properties of matter allowed it to exist at all when in such small masses : e.g. Lillie has proved that there is a minimum size (determined no doubt chiefly by surface-tension) below which pieces of Stentor (a ciliated Infusorium) cannot regenerate. See p. 47.

1] IDEA OF INDIVIDUALITY 11

is stopped for ever. Even in animals with the most astounding powers of regeneration, the working of the whole is always impaired, if only for a short time, by the removal of a part: some regulation, or remodelling, is necessary before the mutilated mass is ready to function as a whole once more. Even such an animal is a whole and no mere aggregate: it has an inner principle of unity, which may be loosely fixed and lightly changed, but is none the less real. Our hypothetical homogeneous masses have, in themselves, no inner principle: their definiteness is imposed on them from without, and one feels that if the external conditions altered, they would have none of the independence of our perfect individual, but would alter blindly with the conditions, like raindrops, which in ordinary showers are small, but in a thunderstorm, under the influence of electricity, run together into large heavy drops showing no sign of their composite origin. One can, in fact, consider the working of any portion without the slightest reference to a whole, and it thus becomes evident that nothing homogeneous can be called an individual. Starting from the just not homogeneous, there can be traced a tendency towards ever greater heterogeneity running up through the series of animal individuals. This was indeed only to be expected. To perfect its independence, the individual, it was seen, had to render its actions precise, independent of each other:

and in non-conscious organisms at least, difference of function always implies difference of structure, so that the more independence—the more individuality—an individual is to possess depends very closely on the amount of heterogeneity of its parts. Look for instance at such an individual as a colony of Termites ("white ants") (cf. p. 142), its defence delegated to one caste, its nutrition to another, its reproduction to another ; the various castes are specially adapted in their structure for their various functions. It is obvious at once that the queen with her vast swollen abdomen full of eggs is a much more effective reproducer than if she had retained any of the structure and mobility necessary to defend or look after herself. The soldiers again could not have been such powerful defenders of the colony if they were to have kept any of the delicacy of mandible required by the workers, the craftsmen.

Another illustration : the accurate grasping powers of the human hand are only rendered possible by its consisting of a number of distinct but co-ordinated parts. The action of grasping is an undivided and a single act, but is only possible because the organ of grasping consists of separate and different parts. The pseudopod of an Amoeba, to take the opposite extreme, has no differentiation of parts: hence the functions it can perform are few and unprecise.

In both these cases, the dependence of efficient

action, and so of independence, is clearly dependent upon a visible and obvious heterogeneity of structure. It might appear self-evident that the organs, the animal's living tools, should have a different structure according to the functions they were meant to carry out, were it not that in man we have the example prominently before our eyes of an enormous number of very special functions being executed by a single organ such as the hand. This apparent exception is due to the structure of his brain, which has given him reason and educability for instinct and automatism. True, he has to be at the trouble of exercising his wits, but gains vast potentialities thereby; the brutes have no toils of learning, but their smooth actions are sadly limited. He has learned to make tools from inorganic materials, and *they* serve as the heterogeneous structures by means of which he can perform all his diverse actions. For specialised functions there must always exist specialised structures; but man through his conscious reason has been able to put off the burden of them from his own substance on to the broader shoulders of inorganic nature. There does exist some corresponding heterogeneity in himself, but not in visible structure: it lies in the diversity of his states of consciousness. These cannot all exist as such at one time[1], but by

[1] For a case of heterogeneous physical *structures* which cannot exist simultaneously, see pp. 110, 113. There the structures must alternate

means of the memory, each can be summoned up as it is wanted. No doubt accompanying them there are physical and chemical differences in the nervous tissue, causing differences of continuity between the various neurones, but this physical heterogeneity is of no obvious or visible kind. The broad differences, the differences that can be felt, lie in the states of consciousness, so that the individual, after advancing a long way in its march towards perfect individuality by means of heterogeneity of co-existent structures, has got to its present position by adding to this a new device, heterogeneity of states of consciousness, which states, through not being co-existent, can be more numerous and more heterogeneous than ever the structures could.

One last attribute of the individual, but a very important one. So far the individual has emerged as "Unity in Diversity." It shows diversity both in what it *is*—its physical structure and the architecture of its consciousness—and in what it *does*—the actions which more truly constitute its real essence. It also has unity, because though all its heterogeneity of architecture is devoted to producing heterogeneity

with each other in cyclical change ; here, the memory obviates the necessity for that. Though two states of consciousness cannot actually co-exist at one moment of time, for all practical purposes memory permits it, as when we say that a man can attend to his profession and write a book upon some other subject "both at once," or as when a chess-player plays a dozen games "simultaneously."

of actions, each one of these only has meaning when considered in relation to the whole. Thus the problem so far has been the relation of the parts to the whole. There remains to be considered the relation of this whole to itself. Since it is obviously the working, the function, which is important in an individual, the structures being only instruments for the function's better performance, this question really resolves itself into the relation between the working of the whole individual at one time and its working at another, later time. This has already been implicitly answered. When we said that the hand and its functioning had significance in relation to a whole, we did not mean merely to a whole which happened to be there at that one instant, but to a whole which had a continued existence in time. When the hand takes up a piece of bread and puts it into the mouth, that action has no significance for the whole man if only that instant of time is considered. Its significance is only seen later, when the bread has been digested, absorbed, and carried to nourish all the hungry parts of the whole individual.

What has been said so far presupposes some degree of continuance in the individual ; a survey of the various kinds of organic individuals shows this continuance to be common to them all, and that too in no limited measure, but as one of the fundamentals

of their existence. Looked at from this point of view,
the individual appears as a machine whose working
has for result no " finished article," the uses of which
do not affect the machine, but merely the continuation
of that same working. The result (and the object)
of the working of a printing-press is to print books :
but the books when printed are of no use to the
press. The result (it is risky to say the object) of
the working of an individual is for it a minute later
to be still working in the same way. There is no
material product given birth to by the process; but
the result of the working is of the greatest interest to
the individual, the machine that is working.

This fourth view of the individual, as a whole
whose diverse parts all work together in such a way
as to ensure the whole's continuance, or, as the
evolutionist would say, whose structure and working
have "survival-value," cannot stand without some
qualification.   There is death to be reckoned with;
the survival is only temporary.

Under cover of the one word Death lie sheltered
two separate notions—death of the substance, when
the living protoplasm ceases to exist as such, and
death of the individuality informing the substance[1].
In man, both are inseparably connected; in many
lower animals they are not. To take the simplest

---

[1] For a fuller treatment of both these conceptions, see an article
on "The Meaning of Death" in the *Cornhill Magazine* for April 1911.

example: most Protozoa, such as Amoeba or Paramaecium, definite individuals both, feed and continually grow, and when they are grown to a certain
maximum size, divide into two halves (see pp.
41, 56), each of which reorganizes itself into an individual
resembling its " parent." Not a jot of substance has
been lost : but one individuality has disappeared and
two new ones are there in its place.

Owing to the material properties and limitations
of her "physical basis" of protoplasm, Life in her
attempt at perfect individuation has been faced by
a dilemma with which she has never fully been able
to cope.

Growth, the balance of gain over loss in metabolism, is either a necessary attribute of protoplasm,
or else, more probably, an easily-acquired property,
of such all-round usefulness that every organism has
seized upon it (see Roux, 16). At all events it is
universal in all protoplasm throughout all or most
of its active existence. Now if Life allows this growth
to take place indefinitely within the limits of one
individual, two awkward things happen ; first of all,
the mere increase of bulk brings difficulties (see
Chap. II), and secondly the increased weight of the
whole needs some kind of a skeleton or scaffolding
for its support. This skeleton, since living protoplasm
itself is not firm enough, must be built out of dead
materials, mere secretions of protoplasm. These have

not Life's power of renewing themselves, of "sprouting fresh and sweet continually out of themselves" like protoplasm, yet all the time are being exposed to the inclemencies of the world and the assaults of enemies: at last something, the oldest part, gives, and involves the whole fabric in its fall[1]. Death of the substance—that has been the result whenever Life has allowed unlimited growth to the individual : and when she preserves the substance, as in the Protozoa, by dividing it into two whenever it has reached a certain size, so keeping the pattern of the race within a narrow range, easily controlled, then there must be death of the individuality. She has never been able to produce an individuality which can for ever keep the unstable structure of its substance nicely balanced against the chance violences of the outer world.

But—and this is important—when the Protozoan divided its substance and destroyed its individuality, two fresh ones sprang up in the two separate masses of substance. The relation of the organism's individuality to its substance will be considered at more length in Chap. VI. Here it can only be said that protoplasm has primitively a great power of self-regulation, so that the plan of the individual's structure which is characteristic for the species can

[1] As examples will serve, the hollow trunks of aged trees, the brittleness of old bones, and the decay of teeth.

exist actual and patent in a given mass of protoplasm, and yet can also exist, though latent and potential only, in any and every part of that mass above a certain minimum size. Break off a Begonia leaf and chop it into little bits ; each bit reveals its latent power, sending roots downward, shoots upwards, and at the last becoming a self-sufficient whole. Through this regulatory power, Life has been able to save herself a tossing from her dilemma, escaping, like a Minoan acrobat, between the very horns : through it she has the possibility of reproduction.

The essence of reproduction is that one individual should create a new individual out of itself. The parent may persist, as in man, after the offspring has come into the world, or, as in Protozoa, may annihilate itself in the very act ; that does not matter. What matters is that in every species there exists a succession of individuals in time, each one derived from the very substance of an earlier, each one built up and working on a common plan. Life has thus been able to steer a middle course. In the higher animals, for instance, she has perfected and used the single individual up to a point, to procure the greatest amount of independence for herself who animates his frame ; then, when it becomes difficult, and more difficult as time goes on, to maintain his supporting tissues in repair and hold balanced the many pro- cesses struggling within him, she calls in the power of reproduction, raises up new individuals of the same sort out of his substance, and abandons him to his fate ; but the race goes on[1].

Our first definition of the individual based on the idea of continuance can now be amended. We must not say that the individual is a whole whose parts work together in such a way as to ensure that this whole, and its working, shall persist ; the individual only persists for a limited time. In spite of this, something does indefinitely continue, though it is but the kind, the species, and not the single individual itself. There is only one kind of working in the species, and this repeats itself in a recurrent cycle ; but for each cycle as it recurs a new individual is required as the instrument of the working[2].

[1] It is to be noted that no actual impossibility stands in the way of the individual's continuance, but only great practical difficulties. Bergson somewhere makes the illuminating remark that the whole of Evolution might have realized itself in a single individual. This, with our knowledge of the potential immortality of many kinds of functioning protoplasm (see Metschnikoff on the age of trees, their propagation by cuttings, etc.) on the one hand, and of the facts of embryology, more especially the striking changes that take place at metamorphosis, on the other, we shall not readily be prepared to deny; but Life, gifted with reproductive powers, has found it come cheaper and easier to choose Death for each single individual and think rather of the persistence of the race than to expend over-increasing energy on patching up the defects that are bound to appear in the individual with age. (See *Cornhill*, 1911, loc. cit.)

[2] It would be more accurate to say *at least one* individual : often two or more distinct and unlike individuals are employed in each cycle of working ; see p. 23.

These qualifications, universally applicable though they are to all individuals that we know on this earth are still mere qualifications, not essential to the pure idea of individuality : the perfect individual would be eternal, subduer of time as well as of space. Since, through practical difficulties, Life has not been able to reach this perfection, she has had to content herself with the next best, continuance of the kind of individual instead of the individual itself.

This, however, is alone enough to rule out of court the pretensions of all inorganic constellations to individuality, those even of crystals and of solar systems. The solar system is a whole most definitely "isolated by Nature," heterogeneous, and composed of parts closely inter-related in their working ; what, besides the objection made above (p. 9), which may only depend on our ignorance, prevents our calling it an individual ? This, that its working is not directed to continuing either itself or other systems like itself.

The crystal has no parts, but is homogeneous ; were it not, its working would still betray it, though at first sight its growth and its strange powers of regeneration display it as functioning to preserve a special form. Put in a weak instead of a saturated solution, and it will not simply cease to exist, like an animal placed in unfavourable conditions, but will unbuild itself as busily and regularly as just now it built itself up. Such a combination of two

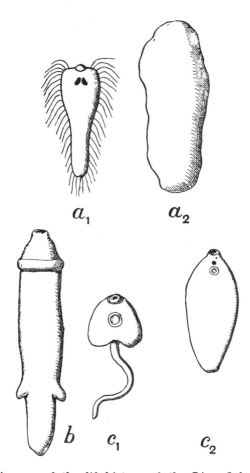

Fig. 1. Diagram of the life-history of the Liver-fluke. The egg
hatches out into a free-swimming embryo (a_1) ; this if it finds its
snail changes into a sporocyst (a_2) ; this produces inside itself a
number of rediae (b) ; which in their turn each produces a number
of cercariae (c_1). These, if conditions are favourable, find their
way into a sheep, where they grow up into the adult Fluke (c_2).
(a_1—c_1, magnified ; c_2 natural size.)

diametrically opposed and equally active tendencies can scarcely be called an individual.

The existence of a species or race, a procession of similar individuals each descended from a previous one, as well as of what we usually call individuals, the separate beings that at any one moment represent the species, leads of necessity to the separation of two distinct kinds of individuality, one belonging to the race and one to the persons that constitute the race. Take as an example *Distomum hepaticum*, the Liver Fluke (Fig. 1). The eggs of this unpleasant creature, which gives sheep the disease known as liver-rot, are passed out of the host and hatch out into minute embryos that swim about in the film of moisture on the meadow-plants. They cannot develop further unless they fall in with a particular sort of snail: if so, they burrow into its liver, and grow up, not into a new fluke, but into an irregular sort of bladder, the *sporocyst*; this, from its inner wall, produces a number of new embryos which grow and burst out of their parent as the so-called *rediae*—individuals differing both from the fluke or the sporocyst. These in their turn give rise to a number of little tailed creatures, the *cercariae*, which migrate out of the snail, pass into a resting stage on blades of grass, and there passively await a browsing sheep. If one by good chance devours them, they hatch out, bore their way into the liver, and grow up again into flukes.

Now each of these three forms that thus cyclically
recur is obviously an individual in the sense defined
by us: they are wholes with diverse parts, whose
working tends to their own continuance, even though
this continuance is limited. But besides this there
is the cycle itself to be reckoned with: it too is a
definite something, a whole, it too is composed of
diverse parts, sporocyst, redia, fluke, it too works
in such a way that it continues (and continues indefinitely). What right have we to deny it an
individuality as real as those possessed by any of
its parts? True, those parts are separated in space ;
but the ant-colony (p. 142) shows that this is no bar
to individuality. The real point is this : the existence of the sporocyst and the redia is of no *direct*
advantage to the individual fluke: it would grow and
lay eggs just as happily if all the host-snails, and with
them all sporocysts and rediae, present and to come,
were exterminated. It is however of advantage to
something, and that something can only be the race
of liver-flukes, the kind of protoplasm which by its
difference from other kinds has earned a special
name—*Distomum hepaticum.*

That is an extreme case; the two kinds of
individuality may often be inextricably interwoven.
What is of advantage to one is usually of advantage
to the other, so that, by an over-emphasis of the
species-individuality of which we are the parts, it

is often said that our bodies are only "cradles for our germ-cells."

It must here suffice to say that wherever a recurring cycle exists (and that is in every form of life) there must be a kind of individuality consisting of diverse but mutually helpful parts succeeding each other in time, as opposed to the kind of individuality whose parts are all co-existent: the first constitutes what I shall call species-individuality, or individuality in time, while the other corresponds to our ordinary notions of individuality and, if a special term is needed, may be called simultaneous or spatial individuality. It is of individuals of this latter class that we have so far been speaking, and to them we must now return.

Our minimum conception of continuance—the continuance of the kind of individual rather than of the single individuals themselves—is thus a touchstone to distinguish between what is and what is not an individual: it now remains to trace the progress of continuance on this earth up towards the unattainable maximum of the undying. At the start, the individual in such organisms as bacteria has a duration reckoned merely in hours or even in minutes. There is but the hastiest procession of never-returning forms across the stage of the species. As we ascend the scale, the individual learns to stay longer and expound his part more clearly. With the attainment of the multicellular condition and the possibility of

reproduction by detaching one small part of himself
instead of by division of the whole (p. 45), he can
even linger on the stage till the next scene is half
played through.

In the actual duration of his life, the individual
ranges from the bacterium's hour to the big tree's
five thousand years. So far the direct and obvious
path can lead. But consciousness once more has
found out a way more subtle and more effective.
Man in this again stands on the pinnacle of individuality—not in mere length of days, but in having found
a means to perpetuate part of himself in spite of death.
By speech first, but far more by writing, and more
again by printing, man has been able to put something of himself beyond death. In tradition and in
books an integral part of the individual persists, and
a part which still works and is active, for it can influence the minds and actions of other individuals in
different places and at different times: a row of black
marks on a page can move a man to tears, though the
bones of him that wrote it are long ago crumbled to
dust. In truth, the whole of the progress of civilization is based on this power. Once more the upward
progress of terrestrial life towards individuality has
found apparently insurmountable obstacles, gross
material difficulties before it, but once more through
consciousness it finds wings, and, laughing at matter,
flies over lightly where it could not climb.

One word more on continuance. The continuance of the working of a species as we have defined it would preclude change; but change and the idea of evolution are at the base of all modern thought in science and philosophy alike. As a matter of fact, the resemblance of the working of one individual to its result, the working of a descendant individual, is never absolute: and so, since working and structure are inter-dependent, no two individuals are ever exactly alike in appearance and architecture. Given this fundamental fact of variation, nothing is impossible: and to-day few would be found to deny that all the battalions of living organisms are descended from one primeval type. That is the logical outcome of the doctrine of Evolution. Evolution is a word glibly used, but often without thought of its full meaning. If Evolution has taken place, then species are no more constant or permanent than individuals. We know what we mean when we use the words child and man, and we know that at puberty comes the crisis which transforms the one into the other; but the whole process is continuous. So we know what we mean by a species; probably, too, there are crises when the species becomes unstable and in a short time we can say, "here is a new species." None the less the one species, if we accept the idea of Evolution, is continuous with the other by the most obvious continuity, that of its substance. As individual emerges from individual along the line of species, so does species emerge from species along the line of life, and every animal and plant, in spite of its separateness and individuality, is only a part of the single, continuous, advancing flow of protoplasm that is invading and subduing the passive but stubborn stuff of the inorganic.

From this short survey of the types and tendencies of existing individuality, three things emerge. First comes the minimum conception of an individual; the individual must have heterogeneous parts, whose function only gains full significance when considered in relation to the whole; it must have some independence of the forces of inorganic nature; and it must work, and work after such a fashion that it, or a new individual formed from part of its substance, continues able to work in a similar way.

Then comes the idea of the perfect individual— something unknown to our senses, its characters a mere raising to infinity of those enumerated above. Defining those characters in different form, we may say that such a being would possess perfect internal harmony, and perfect independence (in our particular sense) of matter and of time itself.

Lastly, and this is perhaps most important for the present quest, there shows the actual line traced by Life in her progress up towards this perfect individuality. She has had to contend with the

limitations of her own physical basis, and the result
achieved is a compromise; not what she planned, but
what her imperfect materials allowed her to carry
out—the old difference between the poem flashed on
the poet's brain and the same poem on paper, striving
to gleam through the words that build it.
Her track is straightforward at first: she tries
to realize to the full the possibilities of her material
basis, increasing the mere size, the mechanical complexity, and the length of life of her individuals, but at
last there comes a point where she can go no further
forward—the spirit is willing, but the flesh is weak.
So far, range of action has been dependent upon
actual mass of substance, diverseness of action upon
complexity of substance, and length of action upon
duration of substance. Now this direct way is barred:
but she finds out another path. She produces a unique
type of mechanism, of which the most fully developed
type is the human brain, and, associated with it, the
power of conscious reason and of memory. At once
the individuality is released from waiting servile upon
substance. Now to its own size it can add the size of
all its tools and machines—by them now is measured
the Range of its action : the Diversity of its action it
has multiplied a hundredfold by substituting indefinite
potentialities for necessarily limited actualities ; and
the Duration of its action, by the device of language,
now far surpasses the allotted span of its substance.

To such an individuality, one that can thus transcend the limits of its substance, the name of Personality is commonly given. Man alone possesses true personality, though there is as it were an aspiration towards it visible among the higher vertebrates, stirring their placid automatism with airs of consciousness. In man, personality is usually defined with reference to self-consciousness rather than to individuality ; but the power of reflection and self-knowledge is linked up, in our one type of personality at least, with the new flight of the individuality— conscious memory seems necessarily to imply a vast increase of independence, so that it is all one whether we define the possessor of a personality as a self-conscious individual, or as an individual whose individuality is more extensive both in space and time than the material substance of its body.

Personality, as we know it, is free compared with the individuality of the lower animals ; but it is still weighted with a body. There may be personalities which have not merely transcended substance, but are rid of it altogether : in all ages the theologian and the mystic have told of such "disembodied spirits," postulated by the one, felt by the other, and now the psychical investigator with his automatic writing and his cross-correspondences is seeking to give us rigorous demonstration of them.

If such actually exist, they crown Life's progress ;

she has started as mere substance without individuality, has next gained an individuality co-extensive with her substance, then an individuality still tied to substance but transcending it in all directions, and finally become an individuality without substance, free and untrammelled. That for the present must be mere speculation. The Zoologist has strayed : he must return to his muttons and his amoebae, and in the next chapter will begin to consider more closely the actual facts of animal individuality and their probable explanation.

CHAPTER II

THE BIOLOGICAL FOUNDATIONS OF INDIVIDUALITY

THE idea of individuality, in common with most other large biological problems, came to be first considered—as indeed was only natural—from the standpoint of man alone. With the growth of our knowledge concerning invertebrate animals, the ideas thus gained had to be considerably modified, until finally the theory of evolution once and for all justified the more advanced among the earlier thinkers, and showed that in any view of animal individuality as a whole, we must not take man and mammals as the single starting-point whence we could logically work backwards to all the rest of the organic world, but must regard them as an ending instead of a beginning, and, what is more, as but one ending among many. From the single beginning, many lines have branched out to the many endings, and the only logical method is to start from the beginning (where, too, the phenomena themselves are far less complicated) and trace out each line to its ending, instead of trying to bring the various endings into relation with each other. Each ending is only intelligible through its history, and the history of one is different from the history of another.

The one advantage possessed by the anthropomorphic view of individuality (which, as a half-unconscious product of every-day experience, is still held by the great majority of those who are not professed biologists) lies in its dealing with long-familiar things. Since, however, this is a very real advantage to those who are approaching a subject the major part of which is bound to be not at all familiar, "full of strange oaths," and so bristling with new names that "bearded like the pard" is scarce a stretch of metaphor, we shall begin here with man; thence, taking stock of the more obvious facts of comparative anatomy, with the historical or evolutionary idea to aid us, try to extend the conception from man to the rest of the animal kingdom; then

we shall have to show some of the chief difficulties
which attend upon this point of view; and finally,
having thus cleared the decks for action, we shall be
able to take up our subject anew from its historical
and logical beginnings. A normal adult man or woman is an organism,
whose complicated and varied parts are almost all
designed for one end—to prolong the existence of the
whole to which they belong[1]. It is in fact a machine
which has the power of running itself, independent,
within wide limits, of what is happening in the rest
of the world. Unlike our artificial machines, however,
whose working is constant, and whose only change is
one of wearing-down, the running of the organic
machine leads to changes in the actual structure of
the machine, and so to changes in its working. We
develop of necessity, of necessity we age, and at the
last we die. But we remain the same individual
throughout—on that all common use is agreed. Till
death, when we obviously cease to be whatever we
have been before, we preserve our individuality in
spite of all fundamental differences in appearance
and behaviour. But as to our nature before birth,
there the common view is at a loss; its uncertainty

---

[1] Those which do not serve this end (with the exception of some
which appear to be "accidental" by-products due to the interaction
of the purposeful factors) are of course destined to help in reproduction.

has found expression in Milton's words, when to
Limbo he consigns, not "Eremites and Friars" only,
exiled thither for theological reasons, but "Embryos
and Idiots" as well.
The very conjunction of his words will help us out
of the difficulty. In our thought, the idea of human
individuality has become interwoven with that of
personality—a purely mental attribute. Even though
by *embryo* Milton meant *abortion*, the lack of
mentality—of personality and of soul, if you will,
which it shares with the idiot, is the same whether it
be within or without the womb, and he was right in
regarding its fate as a grave theological problem.
But (though the reasons for the defect of mental
power are different in the two cases) an embryo
cannot because it lacks personality be considered to
lack individuality too, any more than an adult idiot
can, although the individuality is no doubt less intense
or perfect than in the normal adult man. It is this
confusion of personality and individuality that raises
most doubts in the mind of the average man as to
the claims of the foetus to be called an individual.
The other chief doubt arises from its incapacity to live
out of its mother's body. But reflection will show
that the embryo is like every other living thing in being
able to exist only under certain defined conditions,
which are merely much narrower for it than for the
adult man and the generality of animals. (See p. 132.)

Thus we can take the individuality of man back before birth to a stage when the embryo ceases to be easily recognized by the naked eye. To trace it still further, the man of science with his microscope and his knowledge of simpler animals must step in. There the ordinary man must pause, and there we will leave the question for the present ; turning now to see how far his anthropocentric notions of individuality radiate out to other living things.

We find that he unquestioningly applies the word to all the familiar creatures of everyday acquaintance, the four-legged beasts and the birds, the snakes and the fishes. This is his unconscious Comparative Anatomy—he recognizes instinctively the community of general plan he shares with them. This unconscious reasoning will carry him still further : he will not hesitate when it comes to snails or insects or worms —in fact, show him anything with a mouth and a stomach and he will dub it an individual. So far, all seems plain sailing.

In reality, this is exactly where all the difficulties begin : without studying the outward form and minute structure of himself and of other animals at all stages of development—without some knowledge, that is to say, of all the numerous branches of the science of Zoology,—it is impossible for him to extend his knowledge of individuality any further, and when he does call Zoology to his aid, he finds that in every

direction it seems to lead to contradictions, raising
difficulties worse than those it lays.   To start with,
he has been considering till now only those of the
lower animals which slip naturally into a scheme
taken from the pattern of Man.   A mustering of all
the clans soon reveals numerous types of animals that
will not fit this frame at all.

There are communities, such as those of bees and
ants, where, though no continuity of substance exists
between the members, yet all work for the whole and
not for themselves, and each is doomed to death if
separated from the society of the rest.

There are colonies, such as those of corals or of
Hydroid polyps, where a number of animals, each
of which by itself would unhesitatingly be called an
individual, are found to be organically connected, so
that the living substance of one is continuous with
that of all the rest.   Sometimes these apparent
individuals differ among themselves and their energies
are directed not to their own particular needs, but
to the good of the colony as a whole.   Which is the
individual now?

Histology then takes up the tale, and shows that
the majority of animals, including man, our primal
type of individuality, are built up of a number of
units, the so-called *cells*.   Some of these have considerable independence, and it soon is forced upon us
that they stand in much the same general relation to

the whole man as do the individuals of a colony of coral polyps, or better of Siphonophora (p. 119), to the

Fig. 2. Portion of colony of *Bougainvillea fruticosa*, magnified. *p*, polyps; *m*, medusae; *mb*, medusa-buds. (From Lubbock, after Allman.)

whole colony. This conclusion becomes strengthened when we find that there exist a great number of

free-living animals, the Protozoa, including all the
simplest forms known, which correspond in all
essentials, save their separate and independent
existence, with the units building up the body of
man : both, in fact, are cells, but while the one
seems to have an obvious individuality, what are
we to say of the other ?

So far we have treated the problem statically, as
it were : when we come to view it dynamically,
tracing the movement of life along its course, the
difficulties do but increase. Take, to begin with, a
simple colony of Hydroid polyps (Fig. 2), and ask how
does this multiplicity of connected animals arise ?
Observation shows the whole stock to be formed, by
a process of budding, from one original individual.
A little lump or knob is seen at one place, which,
growing rapidly, bit by bit assumes the appearance
of the individual whence it has sprung ; it takes its
origin in a small group of cells (not in a single one)
and its growth depends on continued growth of the
substance of these cells, accompanied by their repeated division. By this means, the first individual
produces a second out of itself. Its own individuality
is not lost in the process ; it is, however, impaired,
for though the creature's organization is practically
the same as it was before, yet it is no longer separate
in space, and that part of it below the bud's point
of origin is now the common property of the two

individuals. The second individual and the remaining members of the colony, which are all formed

Fig. 3. Hydra, semi-diagrammatic, showing a bud-rudiment on the
right and an advanced bud on the left. *m*, mouth; *t*, tentacles;
t', tentacles of bud. (Magnified.)

in the same way, differ from their original only as
regards their mode of development and, as a con-
sequence of this, in never having enjoyed a free and
full individuality. The relation of the individuals in
a colony to each other is thus rendered still more
obscure owing to the fact of one being produced out
of another. What was at first nothing but a part
grows up into a new whole.

Budding, though perhaps most striking when it
leads to the formation of a colony, is by no means
restricted to colonial forms : often, as in Hydra
(Fig. 3), the process is completed, and the bud set
free to lead an independent life. Here one individual
has produced a second out of its own substance : the
two resemble each other not less closely than two
individuals bred from the egg, and yet the first has
lost not a jot of its own individuality in thus creating
itself anew in the second.

This fresh creation of new forms from the substance
of the old is what we usually term Reproduction.
Budding is but one of its many methods, and we
must look at some others before we can see its full
bearing upon our subject. First we will take fission,
or division into two halves, a method which occurs in
several groups of the higher animals, though less
commonly than budding. Rarely, as among the
stony corals, are colonies produced through its
means ; usually the two halves part company and each

(a)   (b)   (c)   (d)

Fig. 4. Four successive stages in the division of *Stylonychia mytilus*, a Hypotrichous Ciliate Protozoan, from the ventral surface. (Highly magnified.) The outlines of the mouth and the 17 ventral *cirrhi* (locomoting bristles) are shown. Just before division there appear 17 small processes (drawn black) arranged close together in six parallel rows. These enlarge, spread over the body, and become the cirrhi of the daughter-cells, while the parent's cirrhi (stippled) become displaced and at last completely absorbed. The new mouth-region is shaded transversely. In (*d*), division is not complete, but only one half is drawn. (After Wallengren.)

becomes as perfect an individual as its parent. It is, however, in this relation of parent to offspring that division is at variance with budding. Instead of one individual producing another, here the founder of the race ceases to exist, losing his own individuality in the production of two fresh ones. A glance at Fig. 4 will show that the whole substance and the whole organization of the first individual is separated in division into two discrete masses, each of which is incomplete in possessing only half the normal structure. These incomplete individuals, in the examples we have chosen, and in many other animals as well, do not as one might expect complete themselves by keeping the old half-organization intact and budding out what is missing, but, by a method involving a more radical destruction of the parent's individuality, they remodel their structure by a strange internal mason's-work, turning the materials that but now constituted a half-individual into a whole. From their parent they receive the half of its substance and the half of its organization ; they make a new organization without adding to the substance[1]. Growth subsequently increases their size without altering their individuality or organization, until, on attaining to the prescribed

[1] Or at least without adding more than a very small amount. Normal growth may go on, but the re-modelling goes on still faster. That growth and reorganization are not necessarily connected is shown by the strange facts narrated on p. 145.

limit, they repeat the process.   Division is thus even more important for the present purpose than budding; we have the strange paradox that though each individual hands on the whole of its substance intact to its successors, yet with this perfect continuity of substance there co-exists perfect discontinuity of individualities.

There remains the third chief mode of reproduction.   In considering the hydroid colony, we found that all its members took their origin, by budding, from one single founder.   This founder, though identical in organization with the rest, has yet not had the same origin as they.   Tracing its life backward towards its source, we find it first of smaller size; then comes the stage when its organs are developed one by one, much as in the bud; before this it exists in a form through which the budded individuals never pass—as a small drawn-out ovoid, actively swimming instead of fixed to the ground; before this again it is seen as a round motionless body, built up like a mulberry out of rounded parts, and finally its "fount of life" is revealed in a spherical, inert mass, single and undivided—the fertilized egg.

This fertilized egg is neither more nor less than a cell—specialized, as one would expect, for the discharge of its own particular duties, but still a cell. Here is a further strengthening of our view of the higher animal or metazoan as a colony of units each

comparable with a protozoan[1]. When the method is
traced by which the plurality of cells in the adult
arises from the single cell of the egg—the method,
that is, of cell-reproduction—it is found to be identical
with one of the ways of reproduction in metazoan
individuals, that of fission; the single founder of the
cell-community, the egg, divides the whole of its
substance into two halves, each of which is a new
cell. This is repeated again and again, and the whole
army of cells in the full-sized hydroid are direct
descendants of that single founder-cell. But the
hydroid is itself a founder; and the new "individuals"
which it buds out depend for their growth upon this
same process of cell-division continually repeated.

The paradox is growing yet. Each hydroid seems
in its way a whole; yet it is as well a mere part of a
single greater whole, the colony, and, besides this,
itself composed of units each of which again is in
some sort a whole: and each whole has some claim
to the name of Individual.

One gap still yawns: what was the origin of the
single cell that gave birth to the whole adult organism?
In this particular case, it was a fertilized ovum: by
which is implied that the single cell has arisen from
the total fusion, body and soul, or rather cytoplasm

[1] The animal kingdom is divided into the two primary sub-
kingdoms Protozoa or single-celled animals, and Metazoa or many-
celled animals.

and nucleus, of two other cells, these are technically known as the *gametes*, and their product, the fertilized ovum, as the *zygote*. These two cells have come from two separate individual persons (one male and one female) and their cell-ancestors have been firmly built into the fabric of those individuals' bodies.

This merging of two cells and their two individualities in one (the exact reverse of fission) is the essential sexual act, and is usually known as the *conjugation* of the two cells. It will be considered more fully later (p. 71); here it does not concern us, for, as Weismann and others have conclusively proved, reproduction and conjugation are in their origin totally distinct from each other. In all the Metazoa, however, conjugation is always connected with reproduction, so that the fusion of two cells always implies the production of a new individual. In ourselves, and all other Vertebrates, the converse also is true, that the production of a new individual always implies the previous fusion of two cells—reproduction, in other words, is always sexual: but in very many of the lower Metazoa, though conjugation leads to reproduction, reproduction may occur independently of conjugation. Two examples of this asexual reproduction have been seen in budding and in fission.

Thus the complication introduced by the fusion of the two gamete-cells into the otherwise unvaried succession of cell-divisions does not really affect the present question, the relation of one individual to another. The essential point lies in the continuity of individual with individual. To add the final straw, regeneration comes. Regeneration is usually looked on as something strange, almost abnormal, owing to its not occurring in man or his animal familiars. In reality it is much rather an original property of life, which for special reasons has dropped out of the human scheme of things.

As we descend the vertebrate scale, it is not until we reach the lower Amphibia, such as the newt and salamander, that regeneration becomes at all marked. Even here it is present in a restricted form, and is confined to the restoring of lost organs. A leg, that is to say, or a tail, even an eye or a jaw may be replaced, but the central systems and main lines of organization must be left intact. There must remain a certain central residue of the individual if it is to complete itself.

This in itself points to a vaguer, more fluid notion of individuality than can ever be got from contemplation of man alone, but what are we to say of such things as happen in many of the lower animals? Take first one form of regeneration seen in Clavellina, one of those poor relations of Vertebrates, the Ascidians. Cut Clavellina across in the middle, and (in certain defined conditions) a bud will sprout from the front end of the hinder half, and another from the hinder

end of the front half. As in the growth of the
hydroid colony, the old organization is kept entire
and whole, the new organization is built up in the
bud; here, however, it is not one whole individual
giving rise to another, but one half giving rise to just
that dissimilar half which is its complement. What
is more, both the unlike halves of the original whole
can thus add what is wanting—that and no more—
to bring them up to the rank of wholes again. There
is an old school-boy question about a cricket bat :—
suppose the handle of a bat broke, and a new one
was put on to the old blade. Suppose then that the
blade broke and was in its turn replaced; would the
bat still be the same bat? That is a hard question,
but Clavellina asks a harder still.

From this to the extremes of regeneration, such
as occur among flatworms and protozoa, is another
large step. Stentor, for instance (a protozoan which
happens to be specially convenient for experimental
purposes), may be chopped, broken, or shaken up
into pieces of all sizes and shapes, and every piece,
provided only that it is above a definite minimum
size (less than $\frac{1}{300}$ inch in diameter, and in bulk only
1 or 2 per cent. of a full-grown Stentor), and that it
contains a piece of the nucleus, will blossom out as
a minute but fully-formed individual, which will feed
and grow and be indistinguishable from a product of
natural generation.

By now, all faith in man as a guide to individuality must have been shattered.   In man, an individuality presents itself as something definite and separate from all others, something which animates a particular mass of matter and is inflexibly associated with it, appearing when it appears and vanishing only when it dies.   That idea of individuality is not universally applicable.

In perplexing procession before us there have appeared individualities inhabiting single cells, others inhabiting single cells at the start, many cells (and each of these with some kind of separate inhabitant of its own) in later life: individualities whose fleshly mansions are continuous one with another, no boundaries between: individualities that appear and disappear along an undying stream of substance, the substance moulding itself to each as the water of a stream is moulded in turn to each hollow of its bed: within one individuality others infinite in number, lying hid under the magic cloak of potentiality, but each ready to spring out as if from nowhere should occasion offer.

Nothing remains but to abandon preconceived ideas. We must seek to interpret human individuality not as the one true pattern to which all others must conform, but as something with a history and intelligible only through that history.   We must therefore make for the first beginnings of things and trace their upward progress. For this to be adequately done, the very fundamentals must be explored, and the quest begin with an enquiry into the original and essential properties of living substance.

The biologist, looking at life objectively, finds life then manifest itself as the sum of the properties pertaining to a group of peculiar and complicated chemical bodies which are classed together under the general name of protoplasm.

The form and structure adopted by the lowliest living things at the time of their origin, which then had to serve as the starting-point for all subsequent forms and structures in life, are chiefly due to two properties of these protoplasmic substances—one physical, the other chemical. The first is their colloidal nature, which permits of their sharing the definiteness and resistance of solids with the mobility and quick chemical reactions of liquids. The second is their power of assimilation, their power of building up, out of materials different from and chemically simpler than their own substance, new molecules, identical in composition with the old. Assimilation is molecular reproduction, and is by far the most important property of protoplasm. Whenever an organism performs any action, it must needs do work, expend energy. This energy it procures from the break-down and combination with oxygen of some of the unstable living molecules. Combustion

is here associated with chemical decomposition: the
result is not mere oxidized protoplasm, not protoplasm
at all, but various more stable and more oxidized
compounds. Every action thus necessitates the
destruction of some of the living substance, and were
it not for the assimilatory power, whereby it can pick
up materials from the outer world and force them to
assume a structure and arrangement like its own, all
protoplasm would soon vanish into nothingness.

From these two fundamental properties of proto
plasm we can understand three important and almost
universal qualities of living things[1]. First, their
existence as definite bodies marked off in space and
separate from other bodies, no mere formless collection of molecules, here to-day and gone to-morrow,
like a liquid or a gas; secondly their power of movement; and thirdly their growth, due to their building
up more protoplasm by assimilation than what they
destroy in the production of energy. These three
are all of importance in understanding the origin of
organic individuality. Given cohesion of parts, your
primeval organism is marked off from the rest of the
world. Even though it may be homogeneous, no true

---

[1] *Almost* universal, for it will be seen later that mental powers
have made possible such organisms as an ant-colony, which is not
a solid whole, single and defined in space; and growth and mobility
may be in abeyance for long periods, though always present in some
stage of an organism's life.

system of diverse parts, yet this mere fact of existence as a single and separate material body is a first step towards Bergson's "closed system." In non-conscious animals, indeed, where individuality is bound down within the limits of physical substance, this separateness in space is the only foundation upon which such a closed system could be built. Besides this, it presents itself as a whole unit to the forces of the outer world: living substance thus starts with its foot upon the ladder leading to independence, for its molecules cohere, and all know that union is strength.

Given the complex molecules of fixed composition, and, if of various kinds, existing in a fixed proportion, there will be definiteness of shape and action; and given assimilation—the reproduction of new molecules identical with the old—there is the possibility of continuance for this shape and this action.

Analysed thus far, our organism has revealed itself as very similar to a crystal in its definite boundaries, definite and permanent form, and, we may add, in its capacity for growth. It differs only in having a mode of working as well as a form which is continuous.

The organism, however, has two further properties which make it at once more definite and more independent than the crystal. It is more independent, more self-determining, because it can build up its complicated molecules out of simple substances, and

4—2

because these substances—its food—may be varied to a considerable extent and the end-result, its protoplasm, yet be the same. A crystal on the other hand, cannot build up the complex from the simple —it can only add ready-formed molecules to its substance, and can only use them if they are presented to it in one particular way, in the condition of a saturated solution.

An organism is more definite because its size is defined as well as its form. A crystal will continue to grow without limit if only the appropriate mother-liquor in which it hangs is kept saturated: its form is definite, its size indefinite. It is a fact of common observation, however, that each organism has a typical size—not invariable, but fixed within certain not very wide limits. This again is due to the differences in the modes of assimilation of crystal and living thing. In the crystal, growth takes place entirely at the surface. Its assimilation is purely physical: it assimilates to its own physical state molecules of the same chemical composition but in a physical state different from its own. Capturing molecules from their state of solution, it builds them up on its solid self in such wise that they fit on to the pattern of the already existing structure.

With protoplasm, however, assimilation is chemical as well as physical, and growth takes place by *intussusception*, not by accretion. That is to say, it works with raw materials[1], and these materials, instead of being plastered on to the outside, can and do pass in to the interior, and only there are worked up into those combinations of brick and architect, the molecules of protoplasm. Thus, though the absorption of raw materials must of necessity take place at the surface, the actual formation of new living matter, or in other words assimilation and growth, goes on only in the interior.

As a further result of its partially fluid nature, protoplasm is subject to the laws of surface-tension, and a mass of it will therefore tend to become spherical. But in a sphere, as in any other solid body of fixed shape, surface increases with the square, bulk with the cube of the diameter. When we say that one ball is three times as big as another, we usually mean that its diameter is three times as long, forgetting, or leaving implied, that in surface it is nine times, in cubic content twenty-seven times as big. With our balls of living substance, this disproportion between increase of bulk and increase of surface brings difficulties.

Every molecule in the inner parts of the sphere must have oxygen and food if the whole is to go on living. As the organism grows, that is to say as its

[1] Though, as in commerce, one organism's manufactured article is another's raw material; take as an example the quadruple chain of nitrogen-fixing bacterium, clover, ox, and man.

molecule-population increases, the demand of each molecule is no less, but, owing to the disproportion between surface and volume, the supply available for each is dwindling. The actual materials of supply still exist in unlimited quantity, but the organism cannot get at them. If the English Nation, with population advancing by leaps and bounds, were not able to build harbours and provide dock-labourers as quick as she bred men, all the wheat in Canada, with Imperial Preference to help, would not keep her from starvation, for the simple reason that it could not get in.

So the primeval drop of protoplasm, earliest ancestor of all living organisms, the English Nation not forgotten, found, as it grew, its ports and landing facilities not keeping pace with the demands upon them. Each particle of food and oxygen has to be handled by the surface molecules—unloaded from the circumambient water, loaded up again into solution in the general protoplasm—before the central populace can feed or work ; and for each four-fold increase of the transport workers there is a sixteen-fold increase within of the mouths to be fed. This cannot go on indefinitely : but what is to be done?

There are two alternatives. One is for the mass of protoplasm to continue its growth, but obviate the difficulty by spreading itself out in one plane. In such a film of uniform thickness, whatever its extent,

surface and volume will increase in almost equal
proportion. This method, though it has been used
here and there, is not easy of adoption, nor wholly
satisfactory when adopted. To obtain a thin film
instead of an approximately spherical mass of protoplasm, the surface-tension must be very materially
altered, and this implies a deep and continuous
change in the condition of the surface layer as the
size of the whole increases. For main result, the
method has the suppression or at least the delaying
of reproduction. Logically it leads to unlimited
growth of the single mass of living matter, so putting
all the eggs of the species in one basket ; and even
though it is certain that in such a flimsy unco-ordinated
film parts would at length be accidentally torn off or
simply pull apart from the main body, so reproducing
and dispersing the species, yet this reproduction
would be long delayed, and the change of structure
which involved the delay would have brought few
compensating advantages.

The other method is probably easier of adoption,
certainly more beneficial in immediate result. It
consists in this, that the disproportioned mass of
protoplasm divides into two halves. By this means,
though the total volume of living substance is left
unaltered, the total surface it exposes is increased by
over 50 per cent., and the two halves can thus go
on gaily growing until the time comes to repeat the

process. The actual division seems to be effected by a mere temporary lessening of surface-tension in certain regions, so that this would probably be the way of least resistance for the organism, the way that involved less deep-seated change than the first method. In its results it is certainly better. The species (by which is meant simply the kind of protoplasm), by the repeated formation and subsequent wandering away of new separate masses of protoplasm, is widely dispersed, so that it no longer presents a single neck by the severing of which some Nero of an accident could with one stroke exterminate the race.

It is thus almost entirely a direct result of the essential properties of protoplasm, scarcely at all an adaptation to outer conditions, that the earliest forms of life defined and limited their size ;—in other words, that the first stable phase reached by life in her development on this earth was one in which she manifested herself as a succession of separate protoplasmic units, each formed from the bipartition of a former one, each beginning its existence as a rounded body of definite but always microscopic size, and each gradually growing, while preserving its form, till its volume was about doubled, when it divided and left its two halves to repeat the cycle. These, the primary units of life, are usually called by the name of *cells*[1],

---

[1] Some biologists wish to restrict the term cell to protoplasmic units with a formed nucleus. The nucleus, however, has certainly

and the cell is the historical basis of organic individuality.

Protoplasm at its first appearance was presumably a homogeneous substance; as long as it remained so, these masses into which it segregated, however definite their size, their shape, and their reproduction, were yet not individuals. In their working they are like a host of other chemical substances, blindly forging ahead with their reactions, ceasing if the outer conditions transgress certain limits, continuing the same as long as they remain within those limits. They are not, in the strict biological sense of the word, *adapted* to their surroundings[1], they are not adapted any more than such a cyclical or catalytic reaction as that which takes place in the manufacture of sulphuric acid from sulphur dioxide, water, and oxides of nitrogen. These, much after the fashion of protoplasm

arisen by internal differentiation (p. 60), so that the lowest non-nucleated moneron, the complex protozoan, and the specialized metazoan tissue-cell are all *homologous*, and some word is required which will cover them all. Whether a mass of protoplasm is nucleated or not is of importance, but it is of still more importance to know whether it has arisen by a series of divisions from a primary unit of life, and so whether it is itself a primary unit. Such units we shall here call cells.

[1] It will be objected that the change in surface-tension permitting binary fission is adaptive or purposeful. This is quite true, but the adaptation is concerned only with the race; it is the first step towards a species-individuality. The cells within the species, however, remain unaffected.

as it builds itself up and breaks itself down, the
unstable intermediate substance, nitrosylsulphonic
acid, must continually make, unmake, and remake
itself.   As long as the raw materials are present in
the right proportions, the reaction will go on indefinitely.   So it is with protoplasm : the conditions
under which the inorganic reaction can take place
are merely more restricted, so that for it to continue,
man must step in with elaborate mechanisms to
ensure adequate supplies of the substances concerned,
provision for their due mixing, care for the removal
of their by-products.

Any machinery that protoplasm makes for facili-
tating its reactions it must not only make itself, but
actually out of itself.   So it comes about that any
improvement in working must mean some change in
the structure of the protoplasm, and since improvement usually means division of labour, improved
working brings with it a visible differentiation of
parts in the previously homogeneous cell.   What
was a cell and nothing more is now a cell and an
individual to boot.

Our primitive homogeneous masses of protoplasm,
though all the evidence leads us to assume them, are
purely hypothetical.   Every cell that we know to-day
contains at least three, and probably more, diverse
and mutually helpful substances.   There is the outer
layer, whose primary function is absorption, though

the secondary one of protection is often added. Its surface-tension and its solubility must be such that bodies which adhere to it and dissolve in it are useful to the whole cell as food. Within this outer sheath are two further substances. One, called chromatin on account of its affinity for many dyes, is chiefly concerned with assimilation, with the constructive part of the protoplasm's chemical cycle. Usually it is all massed to form (together with other substances) a definite body or *nucleus*, but in various primitive forms, such as some bacteria and some flagellates, it appears in the shape of minute granules scattered at random in the mass of the third substance, which, constituting the bulk of the cell, is called the cytoplasm. This has as its special duty the destructive part of metabolism; it liberates energy, and uses that energy in doing work, such as locomotion, for the good of the cell as a whole.

All forms of life now living must have had an ancestor which existed under this double form of a cell and an individual, and it is our business now to trace the main lines of this development. Here is no necessity to enter into the causes of change; whether we believe in Natural Selection or Lamarckism, are driven back to Bergson's *élan vital*, or even to a complete confession of ignorance, is immaterial as long as we accept change as a fact   Then our task is merely to trace the change itself in its course and expose what to the best of our belief are the main steps it has taken.

Every organism has a general scheme of architecture which can be seen behind the mass of minor adaptive details. It is easy for instance to recognize the vertebrate plan in such different-looking creatures as a giraffe, a sparrow, and a sunfish, or the insect plan in butterflies and fleas. With such a plan to start from, change may work in three main ways. First, it may run through the variations on the original plan, without introducing any new complication. The different species of a genus, for instance, usually differ from each other in this way. Every one can recognize that polar bear and brown bear and grizzly bear are all built on the same bear-plan, though no one can say that one is better, more differentiated, than another. In the second way the original type of plan is retained, but complications are introduced which imply true differentiation of parts and division of labour ; such parts have never been free and independent, so that the division of labour is very different, in origin especially, from that of insect communities or our human society, where the parts themselves begin as independent individuals. This is not mere change for change's sake, but change progressive. We may call this method *internal differentiation*, implying that all has taken place within the original unit. An architectural metaphor may help us. Life finds in the cell the ground-plan for her first mansion—a one-roomed hut. You may change your one-roomed plan from round to square, from square to oblong, and you will not have improved it: but add a chimney and windows, and at once, though still but one room, it is something better. Even a church with its aisles and nave, transepts and choir has grown thus by internal differentiation. In essence it must always be a single room so that the congregation may see and hear the service; and we realize the justice with which the Romans used *aedes* in the singular to mean a temple.

With equal justice they used the plural for a house. They had reached the stage of civilization when a house was no longer a single room, serving more ends than one at once, and all in turn, but a collection of rooms, each one different from any old single-roomed house, all modified in their architecture from being thus built up into a common whole, but none the less obviously separate rooms, each in itself a unit, each somehow comparable with the single space of the more primitive dwelling. This way, of joining unit with unit, is the third way with organic change. Suppose that instead of separating from each other after each division, the cells remain connected. The result will be a colony of cells each one like all its fellows. If division of labour sets in later among the cells, they are rendered mutually dependent, and the colony is transformed into a true individual, which is obviously of a higher order than the cell. It has attained what may be termed the second grade of individuality.

This method, for want of a better term, I shall call *aggregate differentiation*, to show that the individual formed by its means consists of an aggregation of smaller individuals. It differs from the second method in that division of labour, instead of taking place among the parts of a single unit, affects whole units or even groups of whole units.

This third method is of special importance for the evolution of life because those organisms that have adopted it have found the only satisfactory solution of that besetting problem—how to become large. It is of importance for the understanding of individuality because it gives the clue to many of the apparent paradoxes of the higher organisms or Metazoa—why they are built up of units comparable with free-living Protozoa, why they so often reproduce by means of a single cell, why the embryo produced from this single cell so often consists of a number of almost identical cells among which division of labour only later sets in.

Now that the animal has separate units to build with, each with a firm membrane and definite shape of its own, progress is much more rapid. In the first place, metabolism can be maintained in spite of increased size, since conducting channels for the food and waste-products can be constructed.

This would be all but impossible within the limits of an enlarged single cell, owing to the semi-fluid nature of its protoplasm; but now since each cell has a firm outer wall, by joining cell to cell tubes can be made through which the food and the waste-products can quickly pass from end to end of the organism instead of having to work gradually through by diffusion. At first, as in flatworms, most of the various systems of the body—the digestive, the genital, and the excretory—are themselves profusely branched, but later the whole business of distribution and collection is taken over by the circulatory system: this alone is ramified and the others can pursue their more proper avocations in peace[1].

The nervous system is another which can be much more easily perfected in an individual of the second grade. To perform complicated actions which

[1] There is in many protozoa a form of circulation known as cyclosis, in which the whole inner part of the cell is constantly revolving. This certainly performs the same general functions for the organism as does a blood-system, but to have the *whole* of one's inside always in motion would render difficult the development of other systems; thus a huge single cell with cyclosis would have overcome the difficulty of metabolism, but would be at a disadvantage in other ways when compared with a multicellular organism of the same size.

shall be appropriate to the circumstances, there must exist a nervous mechanism consisting of various parts, each part capable of being connected up with every other part. To evolve such a mechanism from a homogeneous mass of substance would no doubt be possible, but to evolve it from a collection of cells would be certainly easier, for there at the outset some of the essentials of the finished product—the separate parts and their discontinuity—would be already given.

Thus through reaching the second grade of individuality, life has been able to gain both size and brain-power for herself. And so it comes to pass that the next steps in her progress have been effected chiefly by the way of internal differentiation. All three ways of change were open to her, and all three have been used in their measure: but the main difficulty, the difficulty of size, has been removed from the path, and the second method can now show its full possibilities. As a matter of fact, the animals of largest size, of greatest intellect, and of best instinctive powers are all individuals of the second grade[1]. At the last, however, when the brain and sense-organs are sufficiently developed, life has gained her most elaborate triumphs of individuality

[1] In the vegetable kingdom, things are somewhat different, and the largest plants, the great forest trees, are individuals of a grade higher again than the second.

by a return to the third method, of aggregate differentiation. How the method is now modified owing to the possession of a highly-developed brain by the units with which it works, will be treated of in Chap. V : every age has known and wondered at the results it has produced—the communities of bees and ants, and the societies of man himself.

Enough has been said to give the stranger in the land a general orientation, and to show him that Life will guide him to a better view-point than Man alone. The main outcome of the enquiry has been to show that living matter at its first appearance on earth, as the direct results of its material composition, could only express itself in the form of cells —rounded masses, microscopically small, each bound, after attaining a limit of size, to divide into two equal halves. Decreed thus by necessity at the outset, these cells are used ever afterwards as the words out of which all life's poems are fashioned. All living things are made of cells and of structures built by cells : all living action is reducible to cell-action. And it was no hyperbole to say that the English Nation is the direct descendant of an ancestor which throughout its life remained a single cell.

The cell was not from the outset an individual : but by its fixed limits of size, its defined shape, and its power of assimilation (by the combination of these properties, be it understood, and not by any

one of them taken singly) it was the first thing
evolved to which individuality could adhere.   It was
like Benjamin Franklin's kite, bringing lightning
down from heaven, but it did more than that, for it
provided a permanent resting-place on earth where
individuality could stay, could gather strength and
develop upwards. For this reason it is right to speak
of the cell as the foundation of animal individuality.
How in later times the relation of the cell to the
individual is modified must be left for the present
on one side (see pp. 137, 150): we must now retrace
our footsteps and see how others have defined the
animal individual.

CHAPTER III

SOME OTHER DEFINITIONS OF ANIMAL INDIVIDUALITY

FROM time to time various definitions of individuality have been given by zoologists. Most
of them are framed with little reference to the
philosophical idea of individuality, and the result
has often been that the term individual as defined
by them, though applicable to some reality of
zoology, can no longer be used without absurdities
in its more popular but more correct and more
original sense.

One of the most widespread definitions considers the individual as "the total product of a single impregnated ovum" (8 *a*, p. 59), that is to say as the sum of the forms which appear between one sexual act and the next. This would make all the polyps in a colony of hydroids, all the separate polyps budded off by a fresh-water hydra, all the summer generations of the aphis, together constitute but a single individual. Of recent years it has not found so much favour, but Calkins (2) has urged that it should apply to protozoa, declaring that all the separate cells arising by continued division from a single parent between one sexual act (conjugation) and the next, should be considered as one individual, no less than the cells of a metazoan like man, which too arise by continued division from a single parent, the ovum, and remain connected to form his body.

Of the various facts which make the hypothesis untenable, the chief are concerned with the artificial or accidental production of two or more co-existent organisms from a single ovum.

In most animals each single fertilized egg gives rise to a single embryo and this to a single adult organism : but in some, where this is the normal rule, more than one embryo may be accidentally or artificially formed from one egg, and in others this multiplicity is the usual course of events, even though most of their relations may grow up in the ordinary humdrum way—"one egg, one adult."

Aberrations may occur even in man : there can be very little doubt that identical twins[1] (to leave all double monsters out of account) arise from the two cells produced by the first division of a single fertilized ovum, which have accidentally been torn apart instead of staying united.

A very interesting variation on this is seen in the nine-banded armadillo (*Dasypus novem-cinctus*) which regularly produces "identical quadruplets" (14). Most mammals give birth to several young at one time, but usually each grows up from a separate and separately fertilized ovum and each is enclosed in its own set of embryonic membranes. The armadillo's brood, however, like the identical twins in man, has only a single chorionic membrane, and the four resemble each other minutely. Always of the same sex, their measurements are identical ; even the number of plates in their armour is constant to less than 1 per cent., though the range of variation from brood to brood may be 5 per cent. and more[2].

[1] It is well known that there are two kinds of twins: *identical twins*, always of the same sex and almost indistinguishable from each other, and *ordinary twins*, which may be of opposite sexes, do not resemble each other more closely than brothers of different ages, and like them arise from the fertilization of two separate ova by two separate spermatozoa.

[2] It is an interesting fact that the four twins fall naturally into

Then comes Experiment and confirms our conclusions of observation. The egg when it develops
outside the body of its parent (the rule with most
of the lower animals) is at the mercy of the experi-
menter. After it has divided into two halves, these
two blastomeres (as the cells produced by the sub-
division of the egg are called) can be separated
either mechanically or by chemical means. In the
majority of animals where this is possible, the half-
blastomere, that identical mass of substance which
without man's intervention would have formed half
the body of the adult, develops, owing to the mere
accident of separation from its sister, into a whole
body. Even with such a highly organized creature
as the newt this has been accomplished.

The experiment may be carried still further.
A whole jelly-fish (Liriope) may grow up from a
quarter-blastomere, and in sea-urchins a single one
of the first 8, 16, or even of the first 32 blastomeres

two pairs, the resemblance between the members of which is still
more close than that between the four taken together. This taken
together with the fact that the members of the pairs are always
adjacent seems to show that the fertilized egg divided into two
halves, A and B, which did not remain united. Then A divided into
$a1$ and $a2$, B into $b1$ and $b2$, and these again parted company.
These four cells gave rise to four separate embryos, $a1$ and $a2$
forming one pair, $b1$ and $b2$ the other. Thus one pair is descended
from A, the other from B, and the closer resemblance of the members
of a pair is explained by closer blood-relationship.

will make a gallant attempt to develop into a
normal whole; and, though it does not succeed,
its death seems due to mere minuteness, lack of
size, rather than to lack of that internal machinery
which produces the complex adult from the simple
egg.

These facts are a *reductio ad absurdum* of the
theory. It is difficult to consider the two or more
experimentally produced sea-urchins or newts as
constituting a single individual; the four armadilloes
with their one individuality raise more than a doubt;
and with the occasional and accidental production of
true twins in man comes finality. If anything is an
individual on this earth, that surely is man; and yet
we are asked to believe that though the most of us
are true individuals, yet here and there some man
who lives and moves and has his being like the rest
is none, that he must make shift to share an individuality with another man simply because the
couple happen to be descended from one fertilized
egg instead of two. In himself a twin is like any
other man; to say that one is an individual while the
other is not, takes all meaning from the word.

The idea rests partly on a misapprehension of the
sexual process, partly on realities which are of some
zoological importance but have no true bearing on
the idea of individuality.

Until very recent times the sexual process, the

so-called "act of fertilization," was looked on as something which had to be repeated at regular intervals to keep the race going. Somehow it communicated to the organism a mysterious force, which sooner or later dying down must be renewed by repetition of the act. This is by no means a true view of sexuality. To start with, one large group of organisms, the Bacteria, seem not to possess it at all, while here and there in higher groups it has been lost ; the American waterweed (Elodea) for instance, that pest which at one time choked half the waterways of England, started its career in this country by being accidentally imported with American timber, and in all its subsequent development has never been known to form seed.

Lower down, near its first appearance, it is not connected with reproduction at all, as in the Ciliates among the protozoa. Hereto it is not a necessary part of the life-history; Woodruff (20) has recently shown that these animals, which reproduce by fission, may be bred through an indefinite number of generations without conjugation. Enriques, on the other hand (7), has shown that a ciliate which has just conjugated, or in other words received a part of the nucleus of another and joined it with its own, may, before dividing at all, and with this very nucleus just formed by sexual fusion, immediately repeat the

process. These observations show that the sexual act
stood originally in no relation to the life of the cell,
or of the multicellular organism, or of the race, so
that any conclusions with regard to individuality
based on the periodical recurrence of sexual fusion
cannot be fundamentally true.

But though the theory cannot be upheld in its
entirety, yet some of the facts upon which it is founded
are of considerable interest not only generally but
also in reference to individuality.

To start with, the upholders of this theory, such as
Professor T. H. Huxley (8 *a*), base themselves largely
upon the facts of metamorphosis, that sudden change,
from the grub to the fly, from the tadpole to the frog,
that occurs at a definite point in the life of so many
animals. What is perhaps the most remarkable
example of metamorphosis, that of the Pilidium into
the Nemertine, he does not mention, since it was only
established some three years later, but as it illustrates
his contentions better than any of his own examples,
it may be given here.

Many of the nemertines—salt-water worms with
long cord-like bodies—lay eggs each of which develops
into a transparent free-swimming creature, very
unlike its parent, and called Pilidium from its resemblance to a little hat (Fig. 5). The hat is provided
with ear-flaps, and between the flaps there is a mouth
leading up into a capacious stomach.

That is its structure when young : at the close of

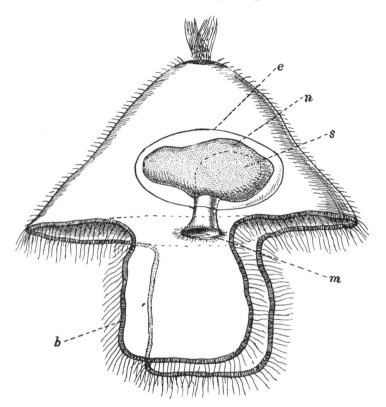

Fig. 5. Diagram of a Pilidium with young Nemertine enclosed. *b*, band of special long cilia; *e*, envelope enclosing the worm; *m*, mouth; *n*, the young worm; *s*, stomach. (Magnified.)

its life, however, it is seen to contain a darker something within itself, and this something on closer inspection turns out to be a young nemertine worm, wriggling actively inside a hollow sac which intervenes between it and the tissues of the Pilidium. This is strange ; but stranger still, the young worm contains within itself the stomach that was the Pilidium's, so that when the Pilidium feeds, the food passes through its mouth into the stomach which is now the worm's. The origin of the worm is equally curious : at a certain stage in the growth of the Pilidium, five little pockets appear on its outer surface, arranged in a ring a little above the brim of the hat. The pockets deepen, and their outer openings get narrower and narrower, at length becoming quite "sewn up," so that there are now five closed bags under the skin. These bags flatten and then extend round the stomach of the Pilidium in every direction, laterally as well as up and down ; they thus meet each other, and the walls which are in contact then disappear, so that all their separate cavities join up into one. There is now beneath the skin an outer shell, then a cavity, and then an inner shell which surrounds the Pilidium's stomach. This inner of the two shells or sacs becomes thickened, undergoes various transformations, and at last gives rise to the body wall and many other organs of the young worm, while the outer sac is merely a temporary protective envelope. The worm at length wriggles so violently as to break through this envelope and the skin of the Pilidium, meanwhile tearing the gullet where it passes from the body of the Pilidium into its own. The worm goes on its way rejoicing, and grows up into an adult nemertine; while the Pilidium still swims about, though stomachless, for a time, but perishes at the last.

A perfect gradation in abruptness of metamorphosis can be traced up to this extreme condition. Often, as in man, development proceeds gradually—a slow transition through continual change. In others, as in the frog, there is one period when a sudden alteration of habit and structure takes place; the tadpole, we say, undergoes a metamorphosis and is made a frog. But though there is radical rearrangement, nothing is discarded. In the butterfly there is a more violent metamorphosis, and also a part of the earlier form, its outer skin, is discarded during the change. Finally in the Pilidium not merely the skin but nearly the whole of the larva is rejected at the metamorphosis.

From this, Prof. Huxley then says, it is but one step for the larva to keep all its essential organs when it parted company with the adult form; the one would be formed by the other after the fashion of a bud, and from this on to the establishment of colonies like those of the hydroid polyps would be but one step more. Then we should have a perfect transition: the animal as it develops is represented first by a succession of forms, each one turning into the one that comes after, but then first a part and finally a whole of one of the forms comes to have a separate existence in space simultaneously with one of the later forms. So, he argues, since the tadpole and the frog can rightly be called mere forms or phases of the same individual, then the Pilidium and the Nemertine, and then all the polyps in the hydroid colony[1], are but such forms too.

As a matter of fact, this gradation does not seem to exist in nature; but even if it did it would not be convincing. It is often forgotten that the most perfect quantitative gradation from one condition to another is no guarantee that the two conditions shall not be qualitatively different. To take the simplest example, when the chemical substance denoted by the symbol H_2O is heated, a definite addition to the rate of motion of its molecules is made for each degree of temperature through which it is heated. This quantitative addition, however, has a qualitative result: with continued heating the substance passes from the solid state into the liquid, and from that into the gaseous, turning from ice to water, from water to steam. There is a similar gradual transition in life from the mere aggregate to the higher-grade individual (Chap. IV).

Here, however, there seems to be no such series.

[1] The examples actually used by him are the Salpae and the Aphides.

All goes well up to the Pilidium, but then comes the gap. There is no case known where two *complete* individuals are formed as the result of metamorphosis. In reality, the detachment of the Pilidium skin from the young worm is not an attempt at reproduction at all, but is due to something very different. This something is the incompleteness of adaptability in protoplasm, and since the subject will concern us again later (p. 132 *et seqq.*) it may be investigated here.

The whole *raison d'être* of a metamorphosis is the restriction of the animal to one environment in one period of its life, to another and a wholly different environment in another period. Different environments require different structures; and the metamorphosis is the time when the old structures are destroyed. When the tadpole, for instance, suffers a land-change, gills and tail must vanish. They do not, like the skeleton of the gills, become converted, after considerable remodelling, into structures of the adult, nor like the caterpillar's outer skin, are they bodily cast off: they are absorbed, they shrink and their contents are drawn into the body of the young frog for future use, as the yolk-sac and its contents are drawn into the body of the unhatched chick.

The tadpole is so well adapted to the water, the frog so well adapted to the land, that certain organs cannot be used, however remodelled, for life on both. They cease to exist as such; it is only the materials

of which they are composed, not the living organs
themselves, which the animal uses for its further
development.

There is a wide possibility of change inherent in
all living substance, but after a certain specialization
of cell or organ is reached, it becomes impossible to
remodel it to perform another totally different function. I say *impossible*: it would perhaps be safer to
say that the difficulty of remodelling becomes so great
that the simplest way, and so the least wasteful of
energy for the organism, is to destroy the old structure,
degrading it to the level of mere food-material, and
then to build up the new from its very beginnings.

An extraordinary example of this is found in the
development of the higher insects. Practically every
organ of the body in a larval form like the caterpillar
becomes broken down, chiefly by the action of
phagocytes, into lumps and masses of dead proteid
substances.

A boy known by repute to the writer once
expressed surprise that there were any organs inside
caterpillars: " I thought," said he, " that they were all
just skin and squash." This would be a very accurate
description of their condition during the metamorphosis, were it not that embedded in the squash at
intervals there lie little patches of living tissue.
These so-called *imaginal discs* are formed of un-
specialized cells ; they grow, unite with each other,

and develop gradually into the structures of the perfect insect.

In the Pilidium, it seems, the young worm finds that less energy is wasted in feeding on its own account than in attacking the larval tissues and converting them into readily assimilable food-stuffs. That part of the individual, therefore, which has been so specialized for a free-swimming life as to defy remodelling for worm-purposes, is discarded altogether instead of being absorbed[1].

As with cells and organs, so with human beings : it is rare that the skilled workman can change his trade. When he is too specialized it may be easier to give him notice and train a new apprentice than to go through the pain and grief of the change from fixed habits.

The remains of the Pilidium then represent merely a part of the Nemertine individual which is discarded as being no longer useful : the history of the process shows that it has nothing to do with ordinary asexual reproduction such as the budding of polyps in a

---

[1] In one species of Pilidium (*P. recurvatum* Fewkes), however, the young worm does actually absorb the remains of the larva. It is interesting to note that a precisely similar series can be traced in the metamorphosis of echinoderms. In the sea-cucumbers the process is almost entirely one of remodelling, in sea-urchins and most starfish the young imago is formed apparently as a "bud" and the rest of the larva is absorbed later, while in some starfish (*vide* J. Müller) the larva and the imago part company.

hydroid colony, and so, even were the detached larval part to regenerate a new stomach and become a separate self-supporting organism (as is not unthinkable) we should not be able to draw any conclusions applicable to colonies produced by ordinary fission or budding.

There is another reality on which, unconsciously, the theory is based. In all Metazoa there is, before and during the sexual process, a shuffling and recombination of the chromosomes of the nucleus—those bodies which taken together appear to determine the characteristics of the offspring, or at least those which mark it off from others of the same species,—whether it shall be tall or short, fair or dark, chubby or lanky, tip-tilted or Roman-nosed. More, it was supposed that this rearrangement only took place during sexual fusion, and instances were adduced of many vegetable "sports," or mutations as they are now often called, so many of which have been enumerated by De Vries. A plant will often appear showing a mutation in all its parts, so that the change inducing the mutation must certainly have affected the single sexually-produced cell from which the whole plant has sprung. Once formed, mutations will persist in cuttings or slips of the parent plant, but will usually be lost when the sexual chromosome-shuffling is allowed to take place and offspring are raised from seed. In such cases then, all the plants that have arisen thus asexually by grafts or slips, from actively growing parts of the one original parent, all possess, in the mutation, a common character separating them from other plants of the same species, and this common difference persists as long as sexual fusion does not take place between bits of their protoplasm.

Phrases such as "he has a marked individuality," or "he is very individual" lead people to suppose erroneously that one of the chief characters of an individual is its difference from all others. Then, seeking for some clue to guide them through the mazes of animal individuality, they seize upon this and say that because one stream of protoplasm exhibits constant differences from other streams, it is therefore an individual. It then appears that in many cases these differences only persist from one sexual act to the next: therefore, say they, the sum of the forms between two sexual acts must constitute an individual.

However, even apart from the initial flaw, that mere difference constitutes individuality, the chain of argument will not hold, for it is found that not all mutations are similar to those we have described : permanent and considerable changes may take place at any time during the life-cycle, and not in the sexual act alone. The so-called *bud-sports* of many plants are of this nature : from a single bud on a

H.　　　　　　　　　　　　　　　　6

normal tree grows out a shoot displaying some new
peculiarity, some mutation which it can transmit to
its descendant shoots. A race of trees with the new
character can thus be raised by grafting, and not
only this, but some bud-sports breed true to seed.
Thus nectarines have repeatedly arisen from peaches,
not only from peach-seed, but also from peach-buds,
and in both cases may subsequently grow true to seed
(4, p. 360).

One last partial justification of the theory is left :
often when more than a single individual life (in our
sense) intervenes between one sexual act and the
next, it happens that these several individuals are
different from each other but appear in a regular
cycle, as in the liver-fluke (p. 23). When this is
so, the forms that intervene between two sexual acts
do in point of fact together constitute an individuality,
one of the type that we have called species-indivi-
dualities. But this coincidence of sexual act and
beginning of a new individuality is only an accident,
philosophically speaking, as our previous discussion
of the sexual process will easily prove (p. 71).

Thus, though we may note as an interesting fact
that the sexual process has at various times and in
various ways become connected with one or another
form of individuality, yet we must recognize that this
connection is not obligatory, that in origin the two
are entirely distinct, and that therefore the one

cannot possibly be used as the basis for the definition of the other.

Another and a very different view is taken by Le Dantec (11), who, sticking to etymology, gives the following definition : "l'individu vivant est donc un corps qui ne peut être divisé sans que l'une au moins des parties résultant de la division perde la vie." This happens, he says, only when there exists a nervous system, and one where the nervous elements are concentrated at certain points to form centres of control and co-ordination, a process which as its climax produces the brains of the higher insects and mammals[1]. Each nervous centre constitutes then in some way the nucleus of an individuality and only animals with highly-centralized nervous systems can properly be called individuals.

The real error of this view lies far back in its premises. The definition contains an error of logic. You may correctly insist on etymology and say that an individual is something which cannot be divided without losing its essential quality : but when you say that the essential quality is life, you are not talking sense. The essential quality of an individual is not life but *individuality*. As a matter of fact, an

---

[1] As a matter of fact there are animals, such as the sea-urchins, where death results from division of the body and yet is certainly not caused by any dislocation of nervous centres, for the sea-urchins have a very feeble and very decentralized nervous system.

individual as defined in this book cannot be cut in
two without its individuality being either lost or
impaired (p. 46); and though the loss may be only
temporary it is none the less real.

Le Dantec's idea, however, is not merely based on
error. The centralized nervous system does form the
nucleus, not of any individuality it is true, but of
that special kind of individuality, a personality.

However, since not *all* brains, but only those
whose mechanism allows some conscious reason and
memory, are the structural tokens of a personality,
and since it is beyond our present power to dis-
criminate between conscious and non-conscious brains
from mere appearance, this structural criterion breaks
down in practice and we are driven to accept behaviour as the only accessible touchstone for
personality.

The same is true of individuality. An individual
is not an individual because it arises from the sexual
fusion of two cells, nor yet because it possesses
a certain aggregate of white fibres and grey cells
called a nervous centre. Even were it a fact that
on this earth these two properties were always
associated with individuals, they would still not
afford the proper basis for a philosophic definition of
an individual. They would be mere accidents of the
individual, which would still owe its individuality not
to them, but to the particular way in which it *works*.

The essential thing about an organism is its actual working, the way it directs the current of energy by which it is continually traversed, and causes it to act on the external world. The main errors of materialism on the one hand and of teleology on the other have resulted from thinking either of substance and structure alone, the mere tools by which the working is carried on, or only of the apparent purpose for which it seems to exist, and not merely of the working itself. Only on this basis can a definition of individuality be attempted, and it is by neglecting this basis that many have been led to false conclusions.

CHAPTER IV

THE SECOND GRADE OF INDIVIDUALITY
AND ITS ATTAINMENT

Question :   " What's one and one and one and one and one and one
                  and one and one and one and one ? "
                                        Alice through the Looking-Glass.
Answer (sometimes) :
              "Each one almost a Whole, yet all but Parts
              They have lost self to form a Greater Whole
              Far nobler than its sum of single Parts."
                                        The Green Bayswater.

IN Chapter II it was shown that the very existence of the first living individual, the cell, was originally

determined by the material properties of living substance. There are large cells and small cells, but,
with few exceptions (see p. 89), it is a very limited
largeness to which even the largest attain. This
limitation, depending as it does upon the surface-
volume ratio, is one of the primitive, original
attributes of the cell ; and to attain size, the cell
must in a way do violence to its nature, somehow
modifying its surface-tension, overcoming its natural
tendency to the spherical, so as to keep its absorptive
organ, the surface layer, large enough to supply the
demands of the inner mass.

Why, however, should the cell not be content to
stay small—what is it to gain from size that it should
strive after it? One is apt to think of size as a rather
unimportant element in life. With the example of
the field-mouse and the elephant, both built so
closely on the same type, the wren and the albatross,
one comes to think of a model of organization which
can be fitted at will on to whatever bulk of living
matter is desired. Within wide limits this is true, no
doubt, but limits none the less there are.

Many Neo-Darwinians, too, argue that adaptation
is the great reality gained by organisms through
natural selection, and that, therefore, no one species
now alive has preference over any other—for to be
alive both must be adapted to their surroundings.
But to exist and nothing more, to vegetate merely,

is not the fate of all organisms. There *is* a higher and a lower, for some are more independent, more powerful than others.

It is now that the importance of size is seen; for increase of size means increase of independence. Most of the forces of the outside world act only on the surface of the organism; but its own forces spring from the whole mass of its substance. The energy necessary for action is let loose by the chemical breaking-down of the molecules of protoplasm and by their combination with oxygen. This, in a primitive cell, is a function of all the molecules, and so of its total bulk. In the higher animals, where locomotive power is delegated to the muscles, the relation still holds good; the three dimensions and so the shape of the thigh-muscles of a jerboa and a kangaroo are approximately the same, and so the surface-volume ratio will hold accurately. If the *length* of the kangaroo is ten times that of the jerboa, then the *surface* of his thigh-muscles will be a hundred, the *bulk* a thousand times as great. Of the outside forces (all antagonistic or at best passively resistant to the organism) that of gravity only is proportional to its mass. If it alone were to be considered, size *would* make no difference to the animal's movements—the weight to be moved would increase proportionately with the forces that were to move it, since both are proportional to the mass of the whole.

In reality, even if we consider locomotion alone, the resistance of the medium—air, water, or earth—in which the creature moves, is equally important with gravity. Everyone knows how much harder it is for a thin, loose-built man than for a close-knit, compact one of equal weight, to make headway in a gale of wind. That is because the pressure of the wind is proportional to the surface exposed, and the thin man, with relatively more surface exposed, has less muscle with which to drive his body onward.

The home of all primitive life was the water; and the resistance of water is immensely greater than that of air. The disproportion between inner and outer force is here so great that it is as impossible to think of any single-celled animal swimming against the most sluggish river as it is to imagine a butterfly poised steady in a twenty-knot gale.

Once more we see the importance of the surface-volume ratio: but what it preaches now is for the organism in direct contradiction to its earlier lesson. Then it said, "thus far and no further, on peril of starvation." Now it warns, "stay thus small, and be condemned to continue the sport of the elements."

How is life to escape from this quandary? She may be content to remain small, like all the present-day Protozoa. Many of these have attained the most amazing complexity for their size; but there are physical limits to the amount of structures that can be contained in a small fraction of a cubic millimetre of substance, and this way has led up a blind alley. One tribe of plants, the Siphoneae, has made a brave attempt to gain size while still remaining a single cell[1]. A plant of Caulerpa, for instance (one of these sea-weeds), may have several square feet of surface, and in spite of being one continuous piece of protoplasm with a wall of cellulose round it, is differentiated into organs resembling in appearance and no doubt in function the stem, leaves, and roots of higher plants. Needless to say, it has only been able to attain this relatively huge bulk by restricting itself to growth in two dimensions only, and is quite thin and plate-like throughout.

What possibilities of development lay along this line we cannot say; all we know is that actually it has not led far. The real advance has been made in a quite different way; by keeping the cell's original form and plan, but joining up a number of

[1] I am aware that botanists distinguish between *cells*, which have one nucleus, and *coenocytes*, or masses of protoplasm with many nuclei, such as are found in Caulerpa and other Siphoneae. However, I am using the word cell in a wide sense, a sense dictated by the historical or evolutionary point of view, to denote a discrete mass of protoplasm isolated by natural causes, and if this definition be allowed, then Caulerpa is simply a single cell which has found out the way to become large. The number of nuclei in a cell is often quite unimportant: in the Protozoa one form may have a single nucleus, while a close relation has several.

them together so that each preserves a considerable measure of independence, and is yet subordinated to the good of the whole. This resulted in the metazoan type of structure, where the individual is built up out of a number of cells instead of one.

As an example of a simple metazoan, we had better take a primitive sponge. Among sponges, *Clathrina blanca* is one of the most primitive. A graceful vase-like creature, pure white, with a long stalk of attachment, and a mere fraction of an inch in length, it obtains its food, like the majority of sedentary aquatic animals, by producing a current. A stream of water can easily be demonstrated passing out of the circular mouth of the vase, and, with a little more trouble, can be seen to enter by a number of quite small holes scattered over the walls. The current is produced by the cells lining the central cavity (Fig. 6): these stand side by side like sacks in a granary, their free upper ends tapering very slightly, and then truncated at the top. The flat top of each is surrounded by the most remarkable transparent cylinder, a mere film of protoplasm, yet beautifully round, and capable of being drawn in at will, or protruded till it equals the cell in length. This is called the *collar*, and in the centre of it there springs from the cell a long vibrating lash or *flagellum*, of uniform thickness throughout, and also capable of retraction within the body of the cell. Usually however it is very much in evidence, beating several times a second, and so producing the current, from which food is taken up and digested by the collar-cells. The bases of these cells rest upon a thin layer of jelly—dead stuff secreted by the living cells,

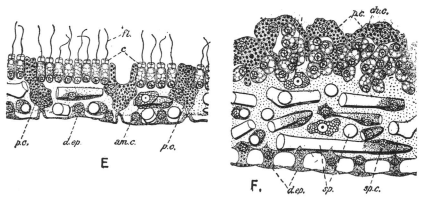

Fig. 6. *Clathrina coriacea*, Mont. Two sections of the body-wall. *E*, not quite fully expanded; the collar-cells line the cavity of the sponge, and show collar and flagellum. *F*, very much contracted. The collar-cells have withdrawn collar and flagellum, and are lying in irregular masses behind the layer of immigrated pore-cells. *am.c*, amoebocytes; *c*, collars of choanocytes (*ch.c*); *d.ep*, dermal epithelium; *fl*, flagella; *p.c*, pore-cells; *sp.c*, spicule-cells. (Highly magnified.) (From Minchin.)

and serving, like the somewhat similar gelatinous tissue we shall see in Volvox, for the common support of the separate cells. On the outside of the jelly is the *dermal* layer of flat polygonal cells, fitting together like a mosaic of tiles. The pores through which the current enters are perforations in the bodies of cells, of a third kind large and contractile, each of which stretches drainpipe-wise from the outer world to the central cavity. Embedded in the jelly itself are other supporting structures—three-rayed spicules of carbonate of lime, and through it wander at will a number of amoeboid cells, having much the same appéarance and functions as our own white blood-corpuscles, except that from their ranks are recruited the germ-cells, male and female; here, therefore, we have the unusual[1] spectacle of the germ-cells being pressed into the service of the individual.

Here is obviously a unity, an individual of a higher order than the cell. Its forms and its functions both depend as much upon the way the component cells are arranged as upon their structure; from an examination of a single one of its cells, or even one of every kind of cell, you could deduce very little about the properties of the ordered whole. That whole is greater than the sum of its parts; for the problem is one of combination, not of mere addition. In spite of this the cells have preserved a very large amount of independence, and indeed do most forcibly present themselves to the mind as bands of beings like ourselves that have voluntarily enlisted under some beneficent tyrant of a general. That analogy,

---

[1] But not unique—e.g. in some colonial Ascidians, the germ-cells of the bud are formed from blood-corpuscles of the parent.

between cells and men, body and state, has been too often and too far pressed; its incompleteness is at once grasped with the realization that no such general does or can exist for the cell-battalions to obey.

What the bond is that keeps them together, what the force that orders them—this is still one of the most mysterious problems of life. We must first grasp the extent to which minor individualities can persist within the major—see how that centralized empire, the body of one of the higher animals, was in its origin a federation, not a tyranny.

In Clathrina, the cells' independence is largely realized by mere inspection. The collar-cells only touch each other with the lower part of their bodies, and when the sponge contracts, as it does in unfavourable conditions, they—after drawing in their collars and flagella out of harm's way—are actually forced over each other, so that instead of a single unbroken layer there is an irregular collection of cells filling up almost the whole of the central cavity. Whether when the sponge expands again they always fit themselves in between their former neighbours cannot well be proved or disproved, but seems at least unlikely.

The amoeboid cells wander as they please, and the outer or dermal cells, though to be of use to the sponge as protective and contractile tissue they must constitute a single continuous sheet, and so seem merged and lost in the one dermal layer they form, yet show themselves still independent in performing their further function, the secretion of the calcareous spicules. As these are required, single dermal cells break loose from association with their fellows, wander off into the gelatinous groundsubstance, and there take up position where the new skeleton is required. Thus, though what they do only has meaning in regard to the whole, the way they do it proclaims them as partially independent beings.

Experiment reveals further lengths of independence—shows the cells capable of veritable insubordination. By means of experiment it has been possible to study the behaviour of the unit parts after the individuality of the whole has been totally destroyed. By chopping the sponge up small, wrapping the bits in the finest silk gauze, and squeezing them, the cells are wrenched from their attachments, and pass through the meshes either singly or at most by twos and threes[1]. By varying the method, one can procure, instead of a mixture of all the sorts of cells, a quantity of collar-cells free from all the rest, and it is their behaviour that concerns us now.

No properly conducted cell, one would have thought, could wish to survive this forcible severance from the

---

[1] This has been done on various sponges, including Sycon, a not very distant relation of Clathrina: see Huxley (9).

whole, the body which we are accustomed to think of
as constituting the basis of the only real individuality
in an animal. These cells, however, are scarcely
inconvenienced. After a short period of shock during
which collar and flagellum are withdrawn, they begin
joining up one with another, forming irregular solid
lumps which, gradually hollowing their central parts,
are soon transformed into hollow perfect spheres,
their walls a single sheet of cells, and the flagella,
now active, beating on the outside. The general
resemblance to Volvox (p. 104) is striking, and is
made more remarkable by the existence of a group
of Protozoa—the collared flagellates or Choano-
flagellata—whose essential structure is identical with
that of the collar-cells ; if one of these artificially-
produced spheres were found in nature, it would
certainly be taken for a colony of Choano-flagellates.

Many of these spheres were kept alive for over a
month, and there is little doubt that if the right food
were found, they could exist indefinitely, though what
would happen with the multiplication of the cells
and the consequent growth of the spheres it is hard
to prophesy. This remains to be tried ; but the
facts as they stand are interesting enough. For
untold generations no collared cells of a sponge have
ever existed except as a subordinate part of a
whole sponge-body ; and yet, if artificially freed
from that "harmonious constellation," they can act

independently, can unite into new societies unlike anything known to exist in free nature, and can there subsist for no inconsiderable time. So much for the independence of the cells : now for their subordination. If, in the experiment narrated above, all the kinds of cells are allowed to remain mixed after their mutual attachments have been broken, we get a result very different from that obtained with the pure collar-cells. First of all, the cells, many of which are still actively amoeboid, and can be seen crawling over the bottom, unite with each other into small lumps and balls. These balls are unlike any organisms known to exist : for, although all their constituent parts are alive, they are without any arrangement and cannot execute any concerted function. Now comes the strange part : this higgledy-piggledy of cells joined up at random is able to reorganize itself, to produce order out of chaos. First of all the collar-cells sort themselves out and form a central solid mass, the dermal cells migrate to the exterior and join up into a single dermal layer. By so doing (though they still resemble no known organism), they have laid down the ground-plan of the sponge, for it is of the essence of sponges to consist of these two layers in this position. The subsequent changes are changes of detail ; cells of the outer layer detach themselves and form the spicules between the two layers. Then the inner mass hollows itself out, and the collar-cells (till now quiescent, with collar and flagellum withdrawn) arrange themselves in a single layer round the cavity, and become active once more. Finally an osculum and pores are developed and the random collection of cells (though by processes not seen in normal development) has become an actual sponge, living and functioning, similar in every way to one that has grown up from the egg.

Of the two experiments, the first is the more surprising, the second the more mysterious. In the first, a new form of life is produced—something capable of living, that is, and yet in its structure unlike any known animal: but, given the large degree of independence possessed by the cells, the rest follows naturally. In the second, however, there seems to be a strange organizing power superior in kind to the powers of the cells themselves—an idea of the whole, informing the parts. Again the image of a general directing his army, even of an architect arranging his materials, springs to the mind: but again, where is the general, where the architect? There is no possibility of anything thus extraneous existing in the normal sponge, still less in the little balls, composed as they are of random cells in random grouping. However, the nature of this directive power we must leave for later consideration (p. 146). Here it suffices to have shown that it exists.

So far the analysis of the simple sponge individual
has shown it to be composed of definite, separate
cells. These in the normal animal have considerable
freedom and independence, both structurally and
functionally. Under the artificial conditions of experiment, this independence is shown to be very
large, inasmuch as one kind of cell at least can live
alone, leading a strange new life, when separated
from the rest of the body. Though the whole sponge
is a true individual, composed of harmonious parts,
yet those parts can themselves behave as harmonious
wholes. So far, their independence is merely stated
and proved ; by their history it can be more or less
explained, for various converging testimonies all
point to one conclusion, that Sponges are descended
from a particular group of Protozoa, and that therefore every cell now forming part of a sponge's body
is derived by an unbroken chain of cell-division
(interspersed of course throughout with sexual cell-
fusion) from cells which existed as free-living and
independent individuals.

On the other hand there does exist a sponge-
individuality higher than that of the cells : to start
with, in the normal sponge all these cells are working
together for a common end, so that every part helps
every other part ; and in the second place, the plan
of this higher individuality somehow permeates all
the cells, so that from any group of all the kinds of

them taken at random a whole new individual will organize itself.

After this examination of such a compound individual, we must now turn and trace the method by which this second grade of individuality has been built up, the method by which the Metazoa have evolved from Protozoa. The step from first to second grade is one of the two or three most important in the whole history of life; yet it has taken place successfully on several different lines, and unsuccessful attempts are many.

Among the Protozoa, as among almost all other groups of animals, many species live in colonies— using the word colony to mean a collection of organisms all similar to each other, and all united either by living substance or by some framework that the living substance has secreted.

Such colonies are not higher individuals in any sense of the word, but it cannot be denied that they already possess certain properties on which the higher individuality can be grounded. A colony, besides possessing a characteristic shape, forms a single whole, separate from all other similar wholes; this separateness, as has been seen, is a necessary basis for the exclusively or almost exclusively physical individuality of the lower organisms. As regards function, however, the members of the colony often retain as perfect an independence as they would have

if living solitary.   Colonial life in such species (which
are always sedentary), appears to be merely a device
for making the fullest use of a place with good food-
supply.   Such spots are few and far between, and are
discovered by rare individuals only ; thus it is of
advantage to retain the descendants of these favoured
few bound together there in colonies rather than
send them off at once into the world with more
chances of failure than of success.

In other colonies, function is not so diffuse, and
there is a function of the whole which is more than,
and sometimes quite different from, the sum of the
separate functions of the parts.   Even in sedentary
species this can sometimes be seen ; in Zoothamnium,
a colonial bell-animalcule, for instance, a touch on a
single one of the animals composing the colony causes
the whole colony to retract out of harm's way.   This
general contraction, common to a number of individuals, though by no means a necessary result of
colonial life, could obviously not occur if the individuals were living separately, however closely
they were crowded side by side.   But it is in free-
swimming colonies that the unity of common function
is most pronounced.   To take the simplest possible
example, imagine two actively-swimming protozoa of
the same species joined together by whatever means
you please.   If free, each would have a similar motion
to the other, but both would be independent.   When

they are joined, however, the motion of the couple is no longer similar to the motion of its two components. Mathematically it is the resultant of their two motions, and as such depends on the way in which the two individuals are attached to each other. If the action of their locomotor organs is not fixed and invariable, it will also depend on the way in which these are used by the two individuals.

Hence for the couple to move, it is essential that the motions of its two parts shall not neutralize each other, but that they shall be co-ordinated to give a resultant motion useful to the whole couple.

Then there is the resistance of the water to be considered, so that before a colonial organism can move effectively its parts will have to acquire a shape, an arrangement, and a mode of action, differing from those which had served them perfectly when they were independent beings.

The further step necessary before the colony can with full right be called an individual is the differentiation of its members so that they perform different functions. As with the primitive homogeneous lump of protoplasm (p. 57) so with the "homogeneous" colony of similar members; both are on the way to acquiring an individuality for themselves, both exhibit features which are the necessary foundations of that individuality, but neither can with justice be said to possess it.

Illustrating these theoretical points, there exist for us, among various other examples, the members of the family Volvocidae,—an old but well-tried object-lesson. These organisms, claimed by botanist and zoologist alike, are members of the Flagellata, unicellular organisms marked off by possessing long whip-lashes or flagella with which they swim. The Volvocidae seem to be a perfectly natural family. They are all free-swimming; they are all colonial, with a framework of transparent jelly common to the colony; they all possess chlorophyll, nourishing themselves after the fashion of plants; and they all have two flagella, a single "eye-spot" and other morphological characters. There can thus be little doubt that they are all descended from a single ancestor who combined these common characters in his person.

The different forms vary very much, however, in the shape and size of the colonies, in the specialization of the sexual elements, and in the degree of individuation of the colonies.

At the base of the series stands Gonium—sixteen precisely similar flagellate cells embedded in firm transparent jelly, joined in definite arrangement to form a flat disc (Fig. 7). The colony thus constituted lives and prospers, nourishes itself, and grows till comes the time for reproduction. Then each cell of the sixteen divides—once, twice, thrice, and four times—into sixteen little ones. Each of the sixteen groups

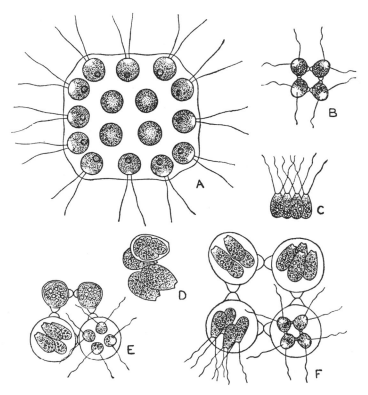

Fig. 7.   *Gonium.*   *A*, a species containing 16 cells embedded in a flat
plate of gelatinous substance.   *B—F*, another species, containing
4 cells.   *B*, *C*, adult colonies, seen from the top and side respectively.   In *D* one, in *E* two, and in *F* all four cells have
divided into four.   The four groups of four cells in *F* will shortly
separate and become independent daughter-colonies.   (Highly
magnified.)   (From West.)

of sixteen breaks away from the rest, arranges its parts in the familiar way, and constitutes itself a minute but perfect new colony[1].

Among all the other members of the family except Volvox, the asexual reproduction (with which alone we need here be concerned) is accomplished in a similar way—each cell takes upon itself to reproduce a whole new colony. They are colonies and nothing more—their members have united together because of certain benefits resulting from mere aggregation, but are not in any way interdependent, so that the wholes are scarcely more than the sum of their parts.

Though, as we have said, Volvox is obviously related to Gonium and the others, it is separated from them by somewhat of a gap.

In the first place, it contains, instead of sixteen or even sixty-four cells, a vast number, mounting up in some species to twenty thousand (see frontispiece). All these cells are inter-connected by fine strands of protoplasm passing through their party-walls[2] and they are arranged in a single layer on the outside of a sphere whose inner parts are filled with a very fluid jelly, so that the Volvox-colony has what we may call an internal medium of its own. Finally, and this is

[1] Some species of Gonium, such as that represented in Fig. 7, are even simpler, being formed of but four cells.

[2] Though these connections have not been described for other members of the family, it is possible that they have been overlooked.

where Volvox has made the great advance, the cells
are not all alike. Most are of the type already seen
in Gonium and characteristic of the family; these row
the colony through the water, steer it, and feed it.
Amongst them, in the hinder half of the sphere,
are larger cells, lacking flagella and eye-spot, and
connected by very numerous strands with their neighbours,

> "Their oarsmen-brothers, by whose toil, safe fed
> And guarded safe, they live a charmèd life
> Within their latticed crystal, peaceably."

And what do they do in return? Now is discovered
the skeleton in the flagellated cells' cupboard—they
cannot reproduce the colony. They are sterile, and
must leave reproduction to the big lazy-seeming cells
who are only lazy, however, because they must store
up food-materials to start the new colony fairly on its
way. They grow and grow, bulge inwards, and finally
come to float free in the centre space, where they still
grow, meanwhile dividing up into a number of cells.
In the end, they become perfect miniature colonies,
burst out of their parent and swim happily away.

Volvox is thus a real individual; of the two kinds
of cells each has given up something the better to
fulfil its own special duty. There is division of
labour, and, from the point of view of the species,
each kind is meaningless apart from the other.

The division of labour in Volvox is that usually

first seen in compound individuals—between the reproductive functions on the one side and all the rest
on the other. In other words, one sort of cell is
concerned entirely with the species, the other entirely
with the separate individuals of which the species
consists; to use the current phraseology, the one sort
is *germinal*, the other *somatic*. The word somatic
opens up another view: Volvox is the first organism
which, in the ordinary sense of the word, has a mortal
body. Its substance is not passed on unimpaired
from individual to individual, but with each act of
generation the major part must die, sacrificed for the
greater efficiency of the race.

In Volvox, this body consists of but one sort of
cell: in all the organisms usually known as Metazoa
there are at least two sorts, if not more. Besides the
division of labour between germ and soma, there is
developed another in the soma itself, at the first
between protective and nutritive cells, the one forming an outer covering round the other, which in its
turn surrounds an internal cavity. But even if Volvox
only possesses species-individuality, the individuality
is none the less real; and the fact that in the family
Volvocidae we can positively affirm that the step from
an aggregate to a higher individual has actually taken
place, is one of the most important in biology.

This, however, is not the only way in which the
second grade can or has been reached. It is quite

possible that division of labour should set in at the very beginning, and that no such thing as a colony, using the word in its usual sense as a number of equivalent individuals all derived from a single parent and still connected together, should ever have existed.

The best examples of animals with such a history are the Catenata, a small group, all parasites of certain marine worms, discovered by Dogiel (6) only four years ago, and containing but one known genus, Haplozoon. The structure of the most primitive member of the group is simplicity itself (Fig. 9, *e*). It is a single row of cells, one end fixed to the wall of the worm's gut, the other sticking out into the gut-cavity. The cells, however, are by no means similar among themselves. The first one takes over all the business of attachment, and most of the nutrition. Actively movable, it possesses at its anterior end a piercing spine and a bundle of delicate protoplasmic threads or pseudopodia, which insinuate themselves far up between the cells lining the host's digestive tube, and serve the double purpose of holding the parasite firm and of sucking up the juices of the neighbouring tissue. From its posterior end this head-cell is continually dividing off new cells, which remain attached to each other in series, up to some seven or eight. The hinder cells of the series gradually become filled with particles of reserve food, analogous to the yolk granules in an egg, and finally lose their connection with the rest, dropping off into the digestive cavity and passing thence to the outer world. Attempts to

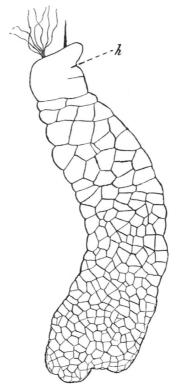

Fig. 8. *Haplozoon macrostylum*, × 300, showing the greatest complexity reached by the Catenata. Only the cell-outlines are drawn. *h*, head-cell with stylet and pseudopodia. A body-cell is being divided off from it posteriorly. (After Dogiel, slightly modified.)

rear them further have not succeeded, but there can

be no doubt that their function is reproductive,
designed to spread the race to other hosts.

That is the simplest form: thence to the most
complex an interesting series may be traced, through
species where a few of the hinder cells divide in such
a way that the animal's posterior end is a plate, not a
mere row, of cells, then up to others where this state
of things begins much earlier, so that the plate is
broadly wedge-shaped, and finally to forms where the
hinder cells divide in all three directions of space, and
the posterior end is large and club-shaped, several
layers in thickness (Fig. 8).   In the front half of the
body, little openings exist between cell and cell, which
serve to pass food-substances down from the "head"
into the other cells.   When these are full-fed, they
close themselves off from their neighbours and pre-
pare themselves for their reproductive destiny.

The ancestry of these curious creatures is almost
certainly to be sought in another group of plant-like
unicellular flagellates, the Peridineae.   These are two
forms which serve to bridge the gap—a large one—
between the active free Peridineae and the parasitic
multicellular Haplozoon.

The first, *Gymnodinium pulvisculus* (Fig. 9, *a*), is
also a parasite but an external one: it is found attached to the skin of various pelagic creatures by a
stalk or bundle of sucking pseudopodia like those of
Haplozoon.   So it thrives till it is full grown: then,

breaking off from its stalk, it divides up into a large
number of little cells each of which develops two
flagella, takes on the form characteristic of the
free-swimming Peridineae, and is off to infest new
hosts.   Here, it will be seen, the same cell devotes
itself at one period to nutrition and at another to
dispersal.

In *Blastodinium mycetoides* (Fig. 9, *b*), these two
functions are carried on by different structural units :
the full-fed cell does not break off from the stalk that
nourishes it, but divides transversely into two halves
which become separated by a membrane.   The one
that is no longer attached to the stalk at once begins
dividing up to form little flagellates, while the other
goes on feeding, grows to full size again, and cuts off
a second reproductive cell.

Now imagine the reproductive cells to remain
organically connected with the stalk-cell and to be
nourished by it for some time after they have been
divided off, and you have in essentials a simple species
of Haplozoon (Fig. 9, *c—e*).

The Catenata and Volvox are thus similar in
being multicellular organisms with unified function
and with division of labour among their parts; but
their origin is very different.

In the making of Volvox, community-life—mere
aggregation—came first, division of labour last.   In
Haplozoon's history, division of labour existed before

any trace of communal existence, and only later was
one cell built up upon another into an individual of
a higher order.

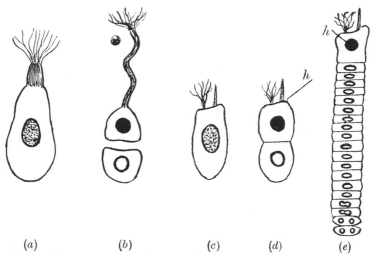

(a)   (b)   (c)   (d)   (e)

Fig. 9.   Diagram to show the probable evolution of the Catenata.
   (a)   *Gymnodinium pulvisculus*, during its nutritive phase.
   (b)   *Blastodinium mycetoides*.   A nutritive cell remains per-
       manently attached to the host, and repeatedly divides
       off reproductive cells from itself.
(c)—(e)   *Haplozoon lineare*.   *h*, head-cell.
       (c)   One-cell stage, resembling (a).
       (d)   Two-cell stage, resembling (b) except that the two
          cells adhere to each other.
       (e)   Adult, with reproductive cells about to be de-
          tached posteriorly.
[Somatic nuclei *black*; germinal nuclei *white*; mixed nuclei
    stippled.]   (Modified from Dogiel.)

To take parallel cases in a different grade of
individuality, the simpler Volvocidae closely resemble

many low human races among which every family
exercises all the ordinary arts and crafts, and where
society, in spite often of strong communal life, can
therefore not rise above the dead level conditioned
by the impossibility of doing all things at once and
doing them well. Curious and interesting it is that
these same peoples if taught, can generally learn, and
learn quickly and well, many arts and industries
before undreamt of among them. The capability was
there, but they had not learnt how to use it: only
by sacrificing some of their multifarious functions
is it humanly possible to advance in the rest, and so
to raise society. As with men, so with cells—a
jack-of-all-trades cannot advance in any, and the
same lesson of sacrifice has to be learnt before the
colony can become an individual organism.

A human illustration for the methods of Haplozoon
may also be found, or at least imagined. Imagine
then a man inflamed with the desire to spread among
a benighted race some gospel of good tidings. Poor,
he prints the books himself ; then comes the question
of sending them forth. It is obviously impossible
for a single man to do one and the other simultaneously. If he goes out to distribute them himself,
the printing will be at a standstill while he is away.
If, however, he can obtain volunteers to distribute
the books, he himself can stay behind and pull off
impressions all the time while a new man goes off

with each consignment. Suppose further that while printing he can instruct the distributors in such a way that they will later be able to do their work more soundly, then there will be collected a crowd of embryo distributors at headquarters, from which the fully-trained ones will from time to time depart.

In the first stage the business is like *Gymnodinium pulvisculus*: then like Blastodinium, and at the last like Haplozoon : the division of labour has come as the first forerunner of the higher development, and this it has done because in both cases there are two special functions to perform which cannot be performed simultaneously by a single individual.

The existence of two mutually exclusive necessities is thus the origin of this type of higher individual : at first the single cell performs them both, but at the expense of not feeding while it is reproducing, not reproducing while it is feeding. Again the sacrifice by a part leads to improvement for the whole; the great fact once discovered that of two cells one can feed for both, the other reproduce for both, and the later steps follow almost as a matter of course.

It is to be remarked that for the two functions of nutrition and reproduction thus to clash with one another, it must needs be that the organism can only thrive in a very special and a very limited environment. An individuality like that of the Catenata is therefore found chiefly among parasites, which exist

in just such an environment; but in the outer world
the conditions are rarely narrow and rigorous enough
to call forth such adaptations[1].

It was the other method, aggregation of similar
units and subsequent division of labour among them,
that opened to life the full resources of the second
grade of individuality. In some colony like Volvox
there once lay hidden the secret of the body and
mind of man.

CHAPTER V

THE LATER PROGRESS OF INDIVIDUALITY

"It is provided in the essence of things that from any fruition of
success, no matter what, shall come forth something to make a
greater struggle necessary."   WALT WHITMAN.

EVERY human being who has passed through the
moral struggle will testify to the truth of these,
Walt Whitman's words, in their own experience :
the biologist will witness that they symbolize as
real a truth in the history of life. Life can never
be in equilibrium. Given the two well-established
facts, that living substance can vary, and that living

[1] To mention two examples, there is the strobila with its ephyrae,
and the Syllids producing their special (epitokous) male and female
forms by division.

things if left to themselves would multiply in rapid geometrical ratio, then change in the *status quo* is inevitable. A state of equilibrium may for a time exist, but every balanced organism is as it were pressing against every other, and a change in one means a rearrangement of them all.

The correlated evolution of weapons of offence and defence in naval warfare is closely similar, though simpler far. The leaden plum-puddings were not unfairly matched against the wooden walls of Nelson's day. Halfway through the century, when guns had doubled and trebled their projectile capacity, up sprang the "Merrimac" and the "Monitor," secure in their iron breast-plates; and so the duel has gone on, till now, though our guns can hurl a third of a ton of sharp-nosed steel with dynamite entrails for a dozen miles, yet they are confronted with twelve-inch armour of backed and hardened steel, water-tight compartments, and targets moving thirty miles an hour. Each advance in attack has brought forth, as if by magic, a corresponding advance in defence.

With life it has been the same: if one species happens to vary in the direction of greater independence, the inter-related equilibrium is upset, and cannot be restored until a number of competing species have either given way to the increased pressure and become extinct, or else have answered pressure with pressure, and kept the first species in its place by themselves too discovering means of adding to their independence. While the balance of power lasts, variation no doubt takes place, but there is no strong necessity to guide it. Once let a large, favourable variation take place in a species, however, so giving it a handicap, and then for its competitors natural selection is at once made more active—they must perish or else adjust themselves by a variation, generally in a similar direction. So it comes to pass that the continuous change which is passing through the organic world appears as a succession of phases of equilibrium, each one on a higher average plane of independence than the one before, and each inevitably calling up and giving place to one still higher.

This digression was necessary to give some explanation of the succession of ever more perfect individualities, and the continual repetition of the same methods in their attainment.

Space forbids more than the merest outline of the developments of individuality after it has attained its second grade. We have seen (p. 64) that the method of aggregate differentiation is now for a time the less important : it still, however, exhibits some interesting points.

To start with, division of labour in colonies of second-grade individuals, as in colonies of cells,

Fig. 10.   Part of a colony of *Hydractinia*.   *dz*, dactylozooid (defensive
person) ;   *gz*,   gastrozooid   (nutritive   person) ;   *b*,   blastostyle
(asexual reproductive person);   *gon*, gonophores (sexual reproductive persons) ; *rh*, hydrorhiza (creeping stolon).   (Magnified.)
(After Allman.)

almost universally sets in first between the nutritive
and the reproductive functions—the somatic and the
germinal.

The Hydroids and their relations give us a series
closely parallel at first, though in a different grade
of individuality, with that of the Volvocidae, but
exceeding it considerably in length. Hydra, one of
the simplest hydroids known (Fig. 3, p. 39), has, like all
others, the power of budding ; but its buds eventually
become detached, so that it never forms more than
a very small and temporary colony. Besides this,
there is no division of labour among different polyps ;
all are alike, and whether they shall reproduce
sexually or asexually is dictated to them by the
external conditions.

Then come the colonial forms : and all of these
show some division of labour. All, for instance, when
ripe, bud off special sexually-reproductive individuals
in the .shape of little jelly-fish or *medusae*. Sometimes any polyp of the colony may be able to give
birth to one of these, but very often the ordinary
polyps reserve themselves for feeding, and special
mouthless polyps exist for the one purpose of budding
off the jelly-fish ; they are the producers of the
reproducers of the colony. It seems to be only later
that the somatic functions, the functions pertaining
to the single colony as opposed to the race, get
differentiated, as in Hydractinia (Fig. 10), where there

are special polyps that defend the colony as well as those that nourish it[1].

All these species are sedentary for most of their lives ; history again repeats itself, for once more it is in the free-swimming forms that the members of the colony have been most modified, most subordinated to a higher individuality.

The Siphonophora, close relations of the hydroids, are a group of beautiful pelagic creatures, which slowly drive their trailing length through the water by an array of pulsating bells. Besides these locomotor organs, there are in the colony organs for feeding, for reproduction, for defence, for offence, and for flotation (see Fig. 11). Most of these apparent organs are really modified individuals, either of the polyp or medusa type. The reproductive "organs" are sometimes detached as perfect jelly-fish ; the swimming-bells and the protective bracts often show unmistakeable vestiges of medusoid structures. The nutritive "organs" are very like an ordinary polyp, but without tentacles, and the

[1] It is interesting to note that in the Polyzoa, another group of colonial animals, there has been a different kind of division of labour. The ordinary animals both feed and reproduce the colony, and defence is undertaken by much modified persons called Avicularia (from their resemblance to birds' heads with snapping beaks). Here the differentiation is between most of the somatic and all the germinal functions on one side, and a single somatic function on the other. In some forms there are no Avicularia, the colonies then consisting of only one kind of person.

defensive organs usually have a structure like that of
the defensive polyps in a hydroid like Hydractinia.
There can be no doubt therefore that the various
" organs " do really represent modified hydroids ; and
as these are themselves individuals of the second
grade, a Siphonophoran is therefore an individual of
the third grade. The same process—the subordination of the lower individualities to a higher—which
we traced from a simple flagellate up to Volvox is
traceable again from Hydra to the Siphonophora : but
the interesting point is that nowhere else in the animal
kingdom is there an unbroken series—a series in
which we can affirm positively that beginning and end
are close relations—of such length. In the majority
of Siphonophora, the persons of the colony have
mostly only a historical individuality: some of them
are sometimes so much modified and reduced that it
has baffled all the zoologists to decide whether
they are homologous with individuals or with mere
appendages of individuals : and in function each is
devoted so little to itself, so wholly to serving some
particular need of the whole, that if one were
separated from the rest, it would appear a perfectly
useless and meaningless body to an investigator who
did not know the whole to which it belonged. There
are zoologists who say it is incredible that the cells
of the Metazoa can be homologous with independent
beings like the Protozoa, impossible that a colony

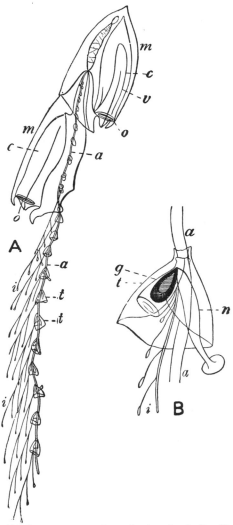

Fig. 11. *A, Diphyes campanulata* (natural size). *B*, a group of appendages (cormidium) of the same *Diphyes* (magnified). (After C. Gegenbaur.) *a*, axis of the colony; *m*, nectocalyx (swimming 'organ'); *c*, sub-umbral cavity of nectocalyx; *v*, radial canals of nectocalyx; *o*, orifice of nectocalyx; *t*, bract (protective 'organ'); *n*, siphon (nutritive 'organ'); *d*, gonophore (reproductive 'organ'); *i*, tentacle (defensive 'organ').

should ever give rise to a single individual of a higher
order than its members (see 5, p. 304). To them we
commend the example of the Siphonophora, and pass
on to consider some other individualities, formed
through aggregate differentiation, but after an entirely new fashion.

To start with, we have the old but ever interesting
fact of *symbiosis*, where two organisms as it were
inter-penetrate, entering into a very close relationship
from which both parties derive profit. The classical
examples of symbiosis are the Lichens, which, long
supposed to constitute a distinct group of plants,
were in the middle of last century discovered to be
actually a mixture of two organisms, one a colour-
less fungus, and the other a green plant—a simple
alga. For the details of their organization any text-
book of botany can be consulted : here it must
suffice to say that there is a perfectly definite arrangement of the algal and fungal constituents. The interesting thing about them is that they will grow, as
anyone can see for himself, in situations which no
other plant would tolerate, so that both plants must
obviously derive advantage from the combination.
Put very briefly, the facts are these : fungi can only
get the carbon of their food from organic matter,
while green plants have the power of using the
energy of light to appropriate carbon from the
carbon dioxide of the atmosphere. In respect of

the absorption of water and mineral salts, however, the fungus seems to be the better equipped. Thus (division of labour once more) the alga supplies

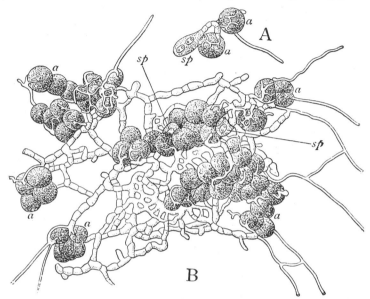

Fig. 12. *Physcia parietina*; building up of the Lichen out of the Alga and the Fungus. *A*, a germinating fungus-spore (*sp*) which has seized upon two cells (*a*, *a*) of the alga *Cystococcus humicola*. *B*, more advanced stage. The spores of the fungus have formed a network in which are embedded numerous algal cells (× 400). (From Scott, after Bonnier.)

carbon compounds for both, the fungus looks after most of the rest of the nutrition, and also shelters the alga from frost and drought.

Algae identical with the green cells of the lichen

are found free-living in spots less exposed than those where lichens grow: the alga, that is to say, *can* exist separately, but in the partnership grows more luxuriantly and has a wider range. The fungus, on the other hand, though it has been grown separately in an artificial medium, cannot develop in nature unless it meets with some algal cells. Fig. 12 shows a young fungus which has just germinated among a group of algae and is now sending forth little tentacles to seize and enwrap them.

The fungus gains more than the alga, but this does not prevent the combination of both, the lichen, from being a very definite individual. A lichen on a barren rock is a something whose continuance as such and in such a situation is dependent upon the co-operation of its two constituents. Here the division of labour is given beforehand in the two kinds of plants, and the new individuality simply arises from the fitting together of these two separate beings into a very close and special relation.

This relation is, however, only a special case of the general relation existing in nature between green plants and all other organisms. Put very crudely, the relation is this:—green plants can build up protoplasm from water, carbon dioxide, and mineral salts : the protoplasm thus formed is the ultimate source of all nourishment to the rest of life. Animals either eat green plants or else eat other animals

that eat green plants ; many bacteria feed on the
dead tissues of animals and plants, bringing about as
a result of their activity the phenomenon known as
decay ; and fungi live to a great extent on the
substances produced during decay. Meanwhile, however, the waste products of the current of metabolism
and the final products of decay, which come eventually to be degraded to simple stable substances such
as water, carbon dioxide, ammonia, and nitrates, get
diffused in the soil, and form the basis once more of
the green plant's activity.

In a sense, therefore, the whole organic world
constitutes a single great individual, vague and badly
co-ordinated it is true, but none the less a continuing
whole with inter-dependent parts : if some accident
were to remove all the green plants, or all the bacteria,
the rest of life would be unable to exist. This individuality, however, is an extremely imperfect one—
the internal harmony and the subordination of the
parts to the whole is almost infinitely less than in the
body of a metazoan, and is thus very wasteful ; instead
of one part distributing its surplus among the other
parts and living peaceably itself on what is left, the
transference of food from one unit to another is
usually attended with the total or partial destruction
of one of the units.

Within this biggest system, nature has been per-
sistent in her efforts to create other "naturally-isolated

systems," other individualities. Out of every little
accidental company she tends to make an inter-related
whole whose parts are largely dependent on each other,
and only slightly on other wholes or their parts.
It will be necessary to give a few more examples
of the inter-relation of two distinct species before
developing this idea. A very instructive example is
that of *Convoluta roscoffensis*, a marine flatworm.
Its story has been so clearly told by Prof. Keeble (10)
that here an outline will be enough. In nature, the
worm is always associated with a unicellular green
plant which lives in great numbers beneath its skin.
The plant on the other hand is found abundantly
apart from the worm, but swarms round the egg-
capsules in order to procure nitrogenous food, and
gets ingested by the young animal. Unless this
happens, the worm cannot develop further—the
presence of the green cells is the only stimulus which
will start its machinery on the next stage of its
working. At first both members gain from the
association, much as in the lichen, but finally, after
the worm (which at last takes no food, but depends
entirely on the surplusage of the alga) has produced
its eggs, it finds itself short of nitrogenous material,
and begins attacking and digesting the green cells ;
they cannot last for ever, and when they are all gone
last of all the worm dies also, trusting to chance that
its young will find new algae. This shows a transition

from symbiosis to parasitism, though the host here
enters the relation of its own free will. Convoluta
somewhat resembles an employer of slave-labour in a
country where slaves are very kindly treated : the
green slaves are well provided for during their individual lives, but they have sacrificed the power of
further perpetuating their species. A growing Convoluta plus its contained green cells is therefore that
anomaly, a temporary individual.

Take next a case of true parasitism. With most
internal parasites, such as trypanosomes (the flagellates which cause sleeping-sickness and other diseases),
or tapeworms, each species of parasite is confined
normally to one host-species, and cannot come to
perfection elsewhere. It is. often extraordinarily
closely adapted to its environment both in structure
and life-history, as a study of any tapeworm will
show ; but that environment is an extremely limited
one.

After this consider an apparently very remote
subject—the relation between insects and flowers.
I need here merely point out that many insects, such as
bees and butterflies, procure all their food from the
honey or pollen of flowers, and that most plants with
conspicuous flowers rely exclusively or chiefly on insects for their fertilization, and so for their continuance
as species. Both insect and flower have been radically
modified in structure and appearance through this

mutual relation. Most flowers are fairly catholic in
their tastes, and are adapted for fertilization by a
number of different insects, and the same is true,
mutatis mutandis, of the insects. But sometimes
the relation is a much narrower one, till finally an
insect may be able to get food only from one particular
flower, the flower to be fertilized only by this particular insect. A relation of this degree of intimacy
(though with not quite the same purposes) is found
between the Yucca-plant and a moth of the genus
Pronuba (Fig. 13). Here (for the details I must again
refer the reader to other books; e.g. (17), Vol. I, p. 201)
the Yucca can in nature only be fertilized by the one
agency of the moth : she, when the time comes for
egg-laying, flies to the Yucca, rakes up a large ball of
pollen by means of a unique structure on her head,
and then flies with the ball to another flower ; there
she sticks her long and curiously-shaped ovipositor
into the ovary of the flower, and lays her egg among
the unfertilized seeds inside. Last she lifts the pollen-
ball on to a special hollow on the top of the stigma,
and pokes it firmly down. The pollen fertilizes the
ovules, of which there are about two hundred, and
they start developing into seeds ; meanwhile the caterpillar hatches, and feeds at the expense of the seeds.
However, it only needs some twenty or so before
undergoing its transformations into pupa and moth,
and leaves the rest to grow into new Yucca-plants.

The whole proceeding is of great interest, showing as it does the blind and instinctive nature of the

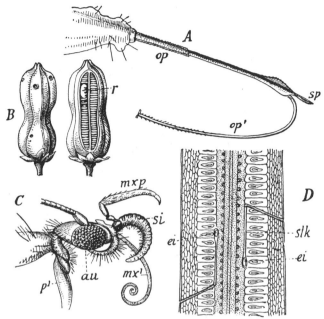

Fig. 13. The Yucca and its Moth (*Pronuba yuccasella*). *A*, ovipositor of the moth. *op*, its sheath; *sp*, its apex; *op′*, the protruded oviduct. *B*, two ovaries of the Yucca, showing the holes by which the young moths escape, and (*r*) a caterpillar in the interior. *C*, head of the female moth, with the sickled-shaped process (*si*) on the maxillary palps for sweeping off the pollen and rolling it into a ball. *mx′*, the proboscis; *au*, eye; *p′*, base of first leg. *D*, longitudinal section through an ovary of the Yucca, soon after the laying of two eggs (*ei*). *stk*, the canal made by the ovipositor.

organisms' actions, and giving us an example of two species absolutely dependent on each other for their

H.   9

continued existence. If the moth had not the structure to form the pollen-ball and the instinct to put it
on the stigma, the ovules would not be fertilized and
her offspring would have no food; and if the plant
was not prepared to sacrifice some 10 per cent. of its
brood, the rest would never develop at all. Here it
is of course the two species that are affected, while
the single moth and the single plant do not depend
on each other in any way ; but the essential point of
the relation—the mutual helpfulness of two unrelated
kinds of protoplasm—remains the same.

Now return and consider these various relation-
ships from the point of view of individuality. The
different species of living things and their members
are all bound up, though but loosely, into a general
whole. Any single species relies on others for some
of the necessities of its existence. In many green
plants this dependence on other species is very slight
and very indirect, while animals, owing to their mode
of nutrition, are always directly dependent on the one
or many organisms on which they feed. None the
less, in nett total of true independence most animals
are far ahead of plants. They have had to make more
effort to get their food, and throughout life, effort
always seems to bring in its train advantages, unfore-
seen and unconnected with the effort's immediate
object. To give an extreme example, the eyes and
ears and other sense-organs of animals were developed

chiefly for the capture of prey and the avoidance of enemies; but once formed, they were the starting-point for the life of consciousness that has culminated in ourselves. A blind deaf-mute child can be fed and live a healthy physical life; its mind, however, scarcely exists:

> "for the book of knowledge fair
> Presented with a Universal blank."

But wisdom at one entrance still can find a way— through the gateway of touch; and the story of Helen Keller, the American girl who became blind and deaf and dumb in infancy, will show how absolutely dependent on external stimulus, even in its dealings with the abstract and the non-spatial, is the mind of man.

The necessity for effort—the "struggle for existence" in the most general sense—has from age to age raised the average level of independence, the measure of individuality's perfection in living beings. In spite of this general rise of level, there has been in every age a falling away, a decline in perfection of individuality in certain species. This decreased independence reveals itself not only as structural degeneration, but also in degeneration's opposite, structural specialization. There is, however, a common cause beneath these opposed effects, and that is over-close adaptation, adaptation to very narrow conditions.

It is self-evident that all organisms must be more or less adapted to their surroundings; in other words they must be more or less dependent upon their environment. Failure to exist in any but a very limited environment is obviously a weakness, a lack of independence, and it seems to be a fact that adaptation to any such limited environment makes it impossible or very difficult for an animal to exist in any other environment. The very success of the adaptation decreases the creature's adaptability.

The adaptation may be concerned only with inorganic nature, as when plants are adapted to conditions of temperature, light and moisture, or only with other animals or plants, or with both. Let us take the second as being most germane to our present purpose. The nutrition of animals falls within this province, since they are always dependent on the protoplasm of other living species for their food. This is a limitation, but its boundary is a wide one. The animal may either make an effort[1] to secure its food, or it may prey parasitically on the labours of another animal. Both ways, if too special adaptation is allowed, may lead to a back-sliding in individuality. We can take a series of examples

---

[1] A metaphorical effort, as when a carnivorous species acquires new powers of speed to run down its prey, or an actual effort, as when the members of that species make use of those powers.

from birds. The Rook and the Sparrow are almost omnivorous, and therefore very independent as regards food-supply. A bird like the Swallow is a little more dependent. In its large gape and strong flight it shows a general adaptation for catching small insects on the wing, but as long as they are insects and small and flying, it is content; it has taken advantage of a common property of many insects, and is dependent in no narrow way. Dependent it is, however, and when the insects fail it must migrate.

Finally, such a bird as the Skimmer (*Rhynchops nigra*) exhibits a very special adaptation indeed. Darwin (3, p. 137) gives a graphic account of them. " The beak is flattened laterally....It is flat and elastic as an ivory paper-cutter, and the lower mandible, differently from every other bird, is an inch and a half longer than the upper." When feeding, "they kept their bills wide open, and the lower mandible half buried in the water. Thus skimming the surface ...they dexterously manage with their projecting lower mandible to plough up small fish, which are secured by the upper and shorter half of their scissor-like bills." This strange bill is without doubt an extremely efficient instrument for catching fish near the surface of the water, but the length of the lower mandible, the very particularity which makes it so efficient for this one purpose, renders it unavailable for any other. The narrow domain where air and water meet it has made its own, but to that one domain it is rigidly confined. The path to parasitism, in spite of apparent differences, is very similar. Here too what the animal seeks is adaptation to an environment which by very reason of its peculiarity and narrowness is not already occupied by other competitors. Eventually the fate of the parasite becomes bound up with that of the host. The final result is thus the same; the form which has made the too-special adaptation loses independence.

Such happenings the phrase-monger will find place for under some vague, comprehensive title such as " Filling a vacant place in the Economy of Nature," and be content. But, though it is undoubted that the pressure of the struggle is always forcing life into these vacuums of vacant spaces, we have to look further before we find what the effect on life will be. Then we see that the process is not always so wholly satisfactory as phrase would make it. In our particular cases the result of " filling a vacant space " is that one species gets preyed upon, and the other, the claim-staker, though gaining the gold in the vacant claim, thereby ties himself down to that little plot of ground, and sinks in the scale of individuality.

Now suppose that the one organism does not merely rush into a ready-made vacuum provided by the other, but that the two should conspire together to create a vacuum of their own, into which, as fast as it is created, they jointly creep. This is in effect what happens when two species become mutually dependent. Here again the relation is at first a general one, as between insects and flowers, but at the last may get very special, as between the Yucca and its moth. Both species here have lost independence. The Yucca, for instance, has to be propagated artificially in Europe, for when it was brought over the moth was left behind, and so no seed can be set. At first sight, then, such a system appears like a double parasitism, and twice the evil that parasitism brings should be its portion. This is not really so, for while the true parasite takes what he can get and gives nothing in return, here each pays the other willingly, for services rendered. In extremes of parasitism there is maximum waste; mutual aid (though it implies mutual dependence) establishes minimum waste. Moth and Yucca together constitute a system which is harmonious and economical because division of labour is at work: each does what it can do best and gives of its superfluity to its partner. If the two parts have sunk in the scale, yet by that very sinking the beginnings of a new whole have sprung up. They have lost in independence, but something else—the system formed by their combination—has gained in harmony. Put in other words, their own individuality has become impaired, but this is compensated for by the formation of a totally new individuality, rudimentary though it be. If the parts of the system, instead of being related by but one tie and for a short space only, were to be brought into relation for the whole of their lives, the resulting system would have the chance of becoming not only more harmonious, but even a more independent individuality than was either of its parts before their mutual adaptation—a consummation actually realized in the Lichens.

This necessity for the parts of a compound individual to lose their own independence for the ultimate greater independence of the whole—this increasing mutual parasitism of the units within an individual—is in fact a brief statement of the main facts observable concerning internal differentiation. Internal differentiation, indeed, to be strictly accurate, is the only way in which individuals are formed, for aggregate differentiation is only a convenient label for the combination of two processes—first the forming of an aggregate, be it of molecules, cells, or persons, and then the welding of this mere aggregate into a true individual by means of internal differentiation.

The progress of the individual of the second grade is in essence a progress towards greater complexity, more harmonious co-ordination, higher independence; this is revealed to the eye in the multiplication and specialization of its various kinds of cells. When it is reflected that these lesser individuals were originally all alike and all self-supporting, the modifications which they have undergone are nothing short of amazing, as a glance at any text-book of histology will show. We can but mention a few of the most remarkable. For shape, the ordinary nerve-cell (Fig. 14) is striking enough; the cell-body is an ordinary, somewhat polyhedral mass of protoplasm, but from it are given off branching processes which divide and sub-divide and with their finest sub-divisions come into contact with the branches of other nerve-cells; and at one point runs out a single thread, the nerve-fibre, which, though its thickness is to be measured in hundredths of an inch, may yet reach a length of several feet before it finds the muscle it is to move or the sense-organ whose message it is to carry. Remarkable in another way are the epithelial cells of our skin, which, continually produced in the deeper layers, undergo a gradual metamorphosis into the thin plates of horny matter called scurf, or scarf-skin; by their perpetual wearing off and replacement from below, they give us an outer covering which shall be at once pliant and sensitive, of considerable strength, and quick-healing.

When an individual's only duty is to commit suicide for the good of the society to which he belongs, the process of subordination has gone a very long way. In what are known as *syncytial* tissues it has gone perhaps still further : here the cells, surrendering all separateness of existence, have fused to form mere sheets of continuous protoplasm studded with nuclei. These syncytia are only the final outcome of a process whose beginnings we saw in Volvox and Haplozoon—the connection of the separate cells by means of strands of protoplasm passing from one to another. These connections seem to exist in all multicellular green plants, and have now been demonstrated in a great number of animals[1]. Many zoologists indeed believe that the fine endings of the nerve-fibrils are always in direct protoplasmic continuity with the organ they supply.

It is worth remembering that the actual history of every individual runs roughly parallel with what we know of the history of the race. Those who cannot bring themselves to believe that the ancestor of a nerve-cell, for instance, was once independent and capable of all the functions of separate existence, often do not consider that every nerve-cell started its life simple, rounded, and undifferentiated, only later throwing out its complex branching processes, and later yet coming into protoplasmic continuity with other cells, originally far distant in the body (Fig. 14).

In many animals indeed every individual epitomizes in its own the history of the race. Starting as a fertilized ovum, an individual of the first grade,

---

[1] See Dobell (5) for facts and references.

it next becomes a "colony" of nearly similar cells,
and then an obvious second-grade individual, with

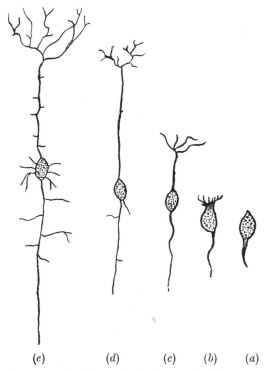

(e)   (d)   (c)   (b)   (a)

Fig. 14.   Five stages in the early development of a nerve-cell from
the brain.   In (a) the rudiment of the nerve-fibre is seen.   In
(c) the dendrite with its branching processes has become obvious.
(e) does not represent the final stage; in the adult nerve-cell
size and complication are many times greater.   (Highly magnified.)
(After Ramon Cajal.)

outer protective and inner nutritive layer.   Then

comes the internal differentiation of this individual :
blood-cells and blood-vessels, nerve-cells and sense-
organs, muscles, sinews, bone, kidney, liver—kind
after kind of cell is created. And let it never be
forgotten that in the embryonic development of any
and every individual all these and many others are
descendants of a single and a simple cell.

It is noteworthy that the course of internal
differentiation has over and over again—in worms,
in insects, in crustacea, in spiders, in molluscs, and in
vertebrates—tended in the same direction—towards
the formation of a Brain. Brain-development has
usually gone hand in hand with the specialization of
other organ-systems—the brain seems a mere bit
of machinery necessitated by the complexity of the
other parts. In the higher insects and the higher
mammals, however, the brain seems to have transcended all the other parts of the body, to have gone
farther than they in specialization, and to be now
in truth the master by whom the rest are to be
employed.

This development of sense-organs and brain has
had great influence on the progress of individuality.
We do not usually stop to consider in what dense
darkness the majority of living things must live and
move and have their being. Without brain or sense-
organs, theirs must be a dim and windowless existence.
The world lies waiting round about ; but it cannot

make its way into their beings. Or say, the world
is locked, and living things must make their own
keys to it. So it is with men : educating their minds,
they forge key after key, each opening a new chamber,
letting in a new flood of light from every material object. Show a flower to an aboriginal savage: what he
sees is something very different from what Wordsworth
or Sir Joseph Hooker would have seen. What he
sees, however, contains more of reality than what
a beetle or a snail, with their imperfect eyes, could
see. The effect produced on an organism when some
object is presented to its senses thus depends partly
on the perfection of its sense-organs, partly on that
of its brain. As we go down the scale, both dwindle :
veil upon veil is let down : till at the last there is an
almost utter darkness, and not of sight alone.

It is this darkness at the base of the animal kingdom which has there made it almost imperative that
the parts of an individual should cohere physically ;
separate them and they would be lost, and could
never enter again into their mutual relationship.
Once produce a sense-organ, however, which with the
brain behind it is capable of clearly perceiving and
accurately localizing distant objects, and it at once
becomes possible to construct an individual, such as
an ant-community, whose parts, though not contiguous
in space, are yet bound together as fast as the cells
of a sponge or the persons of a Siphonophoran; here

as elsewhere the *real* bond is an impalpable one—mutual dependence. The communities of ants and bees are undoubted individuals. Wheeler in a recent paper (18) has abundantly justified this view from a somewhat different standpoint. Here I can only say that if the ideas and definitions put forward in Chap. I are accepted, their individuality is beyond dispute. In spite of space, I cannot refrain from giving one example of the lengths to which internal differentiation of parts can go in such apparently loose-connected wholes. In several species of ants there are special workers whose duty it is to imbibe honey till their fair round bellies are drum-tight, then to suspend themselves, a row of living jars, from the roof, and there to wait until their store is needed by the colony and they are taken down and tapped for general consumption.

One interesting property gained by brains and sense-organs :—organisms possessing them can easily enter into more than one individuality. The Yucca and its moth, for instance, constitute a definite individual that works for its own perpetuation. But their time of contact is a short one ; and there is nothing to prevent the moth from entering into relations with some other flower for the sake of food (in return of course fertilizing the flower) and so forming together with it another " whole with inter-dependent parts working for its own continuance"—another individual.

When we come to man, this power possessed by one unit of entering into more than one individual "at once" (see note, p. 13) becomes very marked. A man can very well be at one time a member of a family, a race, a club, a nation, a literary society, a church, and an empire. "Yes, but surely *these* are not individuals,"—I seem to hear my readers' universal murmur. That is a question which neither the size nor the scope of this book permits. Here we can but express a pious opinion:—that they *are* individuals, that here once more the tendency towards the formation of *closed systems* has manifested itself, though again in very varying degrees, so that some of the systems show but a glimmer of individuality, others begin to let it shine more strongly through. That their individuality is no mere phantasm I think we must own when we find men like Dicey and Maitland (12, p. 304) admitting that the cold eye of the law, for centuries resolutely turned away, is at last being forced to see and to recognize the real existence, as single beings that are neither aggregates nor trusts, of *Corporate Personalities*.

This being so, it yet remains true that the state or society at large is still a very low type of individual: the wastage and friction of its working are only too prominently before our eyes. With the examples of what life has accomplished in producing our own bodies, we can never despair. But we must not be too far tempted by biological analogies : the main problem is the same, but the details all are new. The individuals to be fused into a higher whole are separate organisms with conscious, reasoning minds —personalities ; and the solution will never be found in the almost total subordination of the parts to the whole, as of the cells in our own bodies or the sweated labourer in our present societies, but in a harmony and a prevention of waste, which will both heighten the individuality of the whole and give the fullest scope to the personalities of all its members.

CHAPTER VI

THE RELATION OF INDIVIDUALITY TO MATTER ; CONCLUSION

"Shall man into the mystery of breath,
From his quick-beating pulse a pathway spy?
Or learn the secret of the shrouded death,
By lifting up the lid of a white eye? "
MEREDITH.

A VERY striking experiment can be made on many of those free-living flatworms, the Planaria. If they are cut in two longitudinally, the halves will regenerate into perfect wholes, and this whether they are fed or

not. If not fed they present us with a strange
spectacle (Fig. 15). Without food, they cannot of

(a)   (b)   (c)   (d)

Fig. 15. *Planaria lugubris*. Four stages in the regeneration of a
     whole from a longitudinal half. The dotted line in (a) marks
     the line of the cut. The stippled areas represent regenerated
     tissue. The figures are all drawn to scale. (After Morgan.)
     (Slightly magnified.)

course rebuild their missing block of buildings as we
should, with new bricks: indeed, as energy has to be

expended in the construction, some of the existing
materials must be sacrificed as energy-producers, so
that by the time the bit of worm-protoplasm has turned
itself into a worm, it has actually decreased in bulk
(Fig. 15). The half-worm has never ceased to exist as
a half, but has somehow managed to become an ever
smaller half while remodelling itself continually and
at the same time handing over material for the
building of what is missing. Finally the other half
is completed—a whole worm has been made; up till
now the old half had been decreasing rapidly in size,
the new increasing almost as fast. From the time
that a whole is formed, both halves behave alike,
decreasing slowly together as a result of starvation.

This and many other similar facts tend to show
that the relation of form, and so (since specific form
or structure is only the visible machinery of a specific
working) of individuality in living things to its
physical basis of matter, is primitively a simple one,
though one that is at variance with all our preconceived ideas. It seems to be this: any separate mass
of one kind of protoplasm will be able to, or rather
must, make itself into an individual with the form
characteristic of the species. The only provisions are
that it is neither too large nor too small within certain
defined limits and, of course, that the external conditions are favourable.

Facts suggesting this we have seen in Clavellina,

in Stentor, and in Sycon[1] : indeed, as I have said, it really seems to be an original attribute of life, only more wonderful and startling than ordinary embryonic development because it is no regular part of the cycle of the species. Through its help the animal can extricate itself from positions in which it has never before been.

But, like most other primitive attributes of life, it has undergone considerable restrictions in the course of evolution. Animals, like men, cannot have their cakes and eat them. Three main factors have led to a restriction of this power of regeneration. The first is the formation of different substances for the performances of different functions, and their subsequent segregation into different regions of the body. These substances may get so specialized, so different from each other and from their common ancestor, that one cannot produce the other, and the presence of both is necessary in a mass of substance which is to give rise to a whole individual. In Stentor, for instance, although both nucleus and cytoplasm alike are living Stentor-protoplasm, yet a bit of one without the other will not regenerate. Here the two substances have been segregated by internal differentiation within the cell. Something similar occurs in Sycon, where the collar-cells by themselves cannot regenerate the other forms of tissue necessary to make

[1] pp. 46, 47 and 94 respectively.

a complete sponge; here aggregate differentiation has been at work, and whole cells and tissues are affected instead of parts of cells.

The second narrowing factor is harder to precise; but though we do not know its exact nature, we can often see it at work. There are many animals, such as man himself, where regeneration is almost non-existent although in any given case all the necessary substances and kinds of tissue would appear to be present. Here the failure to regenerate seems to stand in some general relation with the degree of specialization of the tissues; most animals can regenerate more completely when young or embryonic than when they are grown up.

The third factor is more obvious: certain bits of organic machinery are of such a nature that it is physically impossible for the animal to live at all if they are seriously tampered with. It is just because our blood-circulation is so swift and efficient and our nervous system so splendidly centralized that damage to heart or brain means almost instant death to us, while a brainless frog will live for long, and a heart-less part of a worm not only live but regenerate. Thus here again sacrifice is at the root of progress, and only by surrendering its powers of regeneration and reconstitution has life been able to achieve high individualities with the materials allotted her.

But this original property of living matter is

important to us in one way. We begin to realize what an influence the correlation of parts can exert —how one part can affect others by its mere presence or absence. In Stentor, each bit that if separated from the rest would grow into a perfect little whole, remains as a part as long as it is connected with the other parts. If it forms a part, it is because of its relation with other parts; if it forms a whole, it is because it is freed from that relation. Whatever it does, in fact, is due to the tendency of any separate mass of Stentor-protoplasm to form a whole Stentor.

Exactly similar is the behaviour of the blastomeres or separate cells of the segmenting egg (p. 69) only here the subordination is in one way more startling, for each of them is a single cell and represents historically a whole individual. Similarly in all animals where small fragments can reconstitute miniature wholes, the fate of any particular cell in a fragment is determined very largely by its position in the fragment, and would be different if the fragment were of a different size or shape.

This " tendency towards wholeness " thus manifests itself across cell-boundaries as easily as through the more continuous substance of a single cell. More than this, it often seems to disregard them altogether. Many facts of embryology, as when form appears first and cells only later, lead us inevitably to a standpoint resembling that of Whitman (19), when he says of normal development:—"the plastic forces heed no cell-boundaries, but mould the germ-mass regardless of the way it is cut up into cells." Such considerations have led him and several others to throw up the cell-theory altogether, saying that the cells of a metazoan are not homologous with free-living protozoan individuals, but are merely convenient bricks, so to speak, or centres of local government, produced by the forces of life after the form of the creature had been established. But such a conclusion cannot be justified. We must carefully distinguish between what exists to-day, whether in adult body or developing embryo of a metazoan, and what we believe to have happened in the past.

Volvox and Haplozoon, whose cells we can with no shadow of doubt affirm to be homologous with free-living Protozoa, show that it is possible for a higher individual to be evolved from a collection of lower ones. If we refuse to the Metazoa an ancestor formed thus by aggregate differentiation, we are landed in far more and far worse difficulties than any we escape from. Whitman is right in drawing attention to the remarkable fact that the so-called Kupffer's vesicle of embryonic Teleost fish is non-cellular, a mere thin sheet of protoplasm which is not even nucleated, whereas it is certainly homologous with a structure of other vertebrates which is composed of very definite cells, but to reject the cell-theory altogether on this account is not warranted. Rather should we in such facts see examples of the extreme lengths to which the degradation of the individuality of the parts can go—a degradation which we found to be everywhere (except in man's societies) a necessary accompaniment of the formation of a higher individual from an aggregate. Here the cells have become degraded to the level of mere bricks, with even less share in determining the form of the whole than real bricks have in determining the form of a house. But how different is the structure of our Sponge or of Volvox—and they deserve equal consideration with the fish. It is better to believe in the historical individuality of the cells and to wonder at the idea of the whole's form that can thus penetrate the substance and absorb the individualities of its parts, robbing them of all their ancestral freedom, as the universal mind (some would believe) absorbs and loses in itself our souls at death. But here we have come down to the bed-rock questions of biology—the old problems of ordered growth and purposeful working, which are still shrouded in their dense cloud of ancient mystery.

Yet though, like enquirers who try to push far after knowledge in any direction, we are at length brought face to face with the unknown and perhaps unknowable, we have made some solid progress. Without discovering the origin or the inner being

of individuality, we have been able to see it made
objective in the various streams and masses of protoplasm which we call animals and plants, and to trace
an upward progress in its course, at the same time
getting light on many related problems of biology. We
have seen the totality of living things as a continuous
slowly-advancing sheet of protoplasm, out of which
nature has been ceaselessly trying to carve systems
complete and harmonious in themselves, isolable from
all other things, and independent. But she has never
been completely successful: the systems are never
quite cut off, for each must take its origin in one
or more pieces of a previous system ; they are never
completely harmonious, as Metschnikoff's long list
of the "disharmonies" in man will show; and they
are never completely independent. These very
incompletenesses, due to the limitations of the
material stuff with which life has to work, have
proved the foundations of fresh advance. It is just
because every system is bound to be in some degree
dependent, that a number of systems can adjust their
various ways of dependence to each other, till a
condition of minimum waste and maximum inter-
dependence is gradually set up, and a new system,
better equipped than any and all of the earlier ones,
is made.

These systems are individuals, and it thus comes
about that individuals exist in grade upon grade,

any one in any grade being able to combine with others like itself or with others unlike itself to form the beginnings of a new system, a new individual. Moreover, within each grade there may exist individuals of every degree of perfection. At the bottom, a Gonium-colony is but a possibility of an individual; the individual formed by the inter-relation in food-matters of plants and animals is so vague as scarce to deserve the name. At the top, Man astounds by his harmonies, his purposeful completeness, and power over nature ; but none are perfect. Thus we must not expect any hard-and-fast rule; there are many grades, many degrees, and many kinds of individuality, and each individual must be judged on its merits, as something really new.

Finally we have learnt to appreciate the historical point of view, and through it to be brought to admire the seemingly infinite changeableness of life. On the one hand we have seen many structures and many habits of animals that can only be made fully intelligible through their history. Each new species must go through its period of storm and stress while striving to come into harmony with its environment;

> "And 'mid this tumult Kubla heard from far
> Ancestral voices!"

—the forms and patterns of its forefathers rise up and will not be denied, forcing themselves into the altered mould, and thereby often taking on new and unfamiliar shapes.

The ancestral plan may persist in spite of present uselessness, like the elaborate arrangement of the lines of hair on the body and limbs of man; or it may take on some new use, like our Eustachian tube, in fish-like ancestors a gill-slit. It is by this incorporation of the old in the new that we can trace such adventurous histories as that of the cell-individual.

But this persistence is not absolute: with necessity and long lapse of time life seems able to cast away every vestige of the old forms, as when gills are replaced by lungs in air-breathing vertebrates, or when a metazoan structure, once cellular, builds itself without cells.

All roads lead to Rome: and even animal individuality throws a ray on human problems. The ideals of active harmony and mutual aid as the best means to power and progress ; the hope that springs from life's power of transforming the old or of casting it from her in favour of new ; and the spur to effort in the knowledge that she does nothing lightly or without long struggle : these cannot but help to support and direct those men upon whom devolves the task of moulding and inspiring that unwieldiest individual— formless and blind to-day, but huge with possibility —the State.

LITERATURE CITED

(1) BERGSON, H. "Creative Evolution" (Translated). London. Macmillan. 1911.

(2) CALKINS, G. N. "The Protozoan Life Cycle." Biol. Bulletin XI. 1906, p. 229.

(3) DARWIN, C. "Journal of Researches." London. J. Murray. 1888.

(4) —— "The Variation of Animals and Plants under Domestication." London. J. Murray. 1875.

(5) DOBELL, C. C. "The Principles of Protistology." Archiv f. Protistenkunde XXIII. 1911, p. 269.

(6) DOGIEL, V. (Catenata.) Zeitschr. f. Wiss. Zool. LXXXIX. 1908, p. 417 and XCIV. 1910, p. 400.

(7) ENRIQUES, P. (Conjugation, &c., in Infusoria.) Arch. f. Protistenkunde XII. 1908, p. 213.

(8) HUXLEY, T. H. "Collected Scientific Memoirs." London. Macmillan.

   (a) "Upon Animal Individuality." Vol. I. p. 146.

   (b) "On the Agamic Reproduction and Morphology of Aphis." Vol. II. p. 26.

(9) HUXLEY, J. S. (Regeneration in Sycon.) Phil. Trans. Roy. Soc. (B), vol. CCII. 1911, p. 165.

(10) KEEBLE, F. "Plant-Animals." Camb. Univ. Press. 1911.

(11) LE DANTEC, F. "Théorie nouvelle de la vie." Paris. F. Alcan. 1908.

(12) MAITLAND. Collected Papers. Vol. 3, pp. 285 and 302. Camb. Univ. Press. 1911.

(13) MORGAN, T. H. "Regeneration." New York. Macmillan. 1901.

(14) NEWMAN AND PATTERSON. (Armadillo Quadruplets.) Biol. Bulletin XVII. 1909, p. 181.
(15) PERRIER, E. "Les Colonies Animales." Paris. 1881.
(16) ROUX, W. "Der Kampf der Theile im Organismus." Leipzig. 1881.
(17) WEISMANN, A. "The Evolution Theory" (Translated). London. Arnold. 1904.
(18) WHEELER, W. M. "The Ant-Colony as an Organism." Journ. Morphology, 1911, p. 307.
(19) WHITMAN, C. O. "The Inadequacy of the Cell-Theory." Biol. Lectures, Wood's Hole, vol. II. 1893, p. 105.
(20) WOODRUFF, L. L. (Life-Cycle of Paramaecium.) Biol. Bulletin XVII. 1909, p. 287.

APPENDIX A

TABLE TO SHOW THE FIRST THREE GRADES OF
INDIVIDUALITY; AND TO INDICATE THE
DIFFERENCE BETWEEN ACTUAL AND
HISTORICAL INDIVIDUALITY

	(a) Functioning as wholes: *Actual Individuals*.	(b) Functioning as parts, but descended from ancestors that functioned as wholes; thus, though in point of fact not actual individuals, they are morphologically and historically equivalent to them, and may be called *Historical Individuals*.
(A_1) Individuals of the First Grade.	One of the hypothetical non-nucleated ancestral cells (p. 56). A Protozoan. A fertilized ovum.	A tissue-cell of Hydra or Man. A cell of Volvox or Haplozoon. A green cell in Convoluta.
(A_2) Compound wholes made up of first-grade individuals; without division of labour.	Gonium (p. 102).	
(A_3) = (B_0) Ditto, but with division of labour (rudimentary second-grade individuals).	Volvox (p. 104). Haplozoon (p. 107).	

	(a)	(b)
(B₁) Full individuals of the Second Grade.	Clathrina (p. 90). Hydra (p. 40). Man, regarded singly. Pronuba, in certain respects (p. 128).	A single polyp of Bougainvillea (p. 38), or of a Siphonophoran (p. 119). Man, regarded as a Unit of Society. Pronuba, in certain respects (p. 135). Convoluta, considered apart from its green cells (p. 126). A single Ant (p. 142).
(B₂) Compound wholes made up of second-grade individuals; without division of labour.	Many Sponges. Many Corals. Some Polyzoa (p. 119 n.).	
(B₃) = (C₀) Ditto, but with division of labour (rudimentary third-grade individuals).	Hydroid colonies such as Bougainvillea (p. 38). Polyzoa with avicularia (p. 119 n.).	
(C₁) Full individuals of the Third Grade.	Siphonophora (p. 119). An Ant Community (pp. 12, 142). Human Society (p. 143). Yucca-plant plus Pronuba (in certain respects) (p. 128). A Lichen (p. 122). Convoluta plus its green cells (p. 126).	

APPENDIX B

ON THE DIFFERENCES BETWEEN THE CELLS OF THE HIGHER PLANTS AND THE HIGHER ANIMALS

It is probable that in certain points the cells of the higher animals and the higher plants are not strictly homologous with each other.

Botanists distinguish three main types of elementary structure among plants, their differences arising out of differences in the method of cell-division practised (Fig. 16). In the first type

a　　　　*b*　　　　*c*

Fig. 16. Diagram to show the three main types of elementary structure found in plants. (*a*) coccoid, (*b*) filamentous, (*c*) coenocytic. In each case is shown the sum of the changes following upon binary division of the nucleus of a single cell.

(Coccoid), the entire cell, with its cell-wall, divides into two similar and quite separate halves. This is practised, e.g., by unicellular Algae. In the second type (Filamentous), the cell-body (cytoplasm and nucleus) divides as before, but the cell-wall does not divide ; instead, an entirely new party-wall is laid down between the two cell-bodies, and in this partition small apertures are left, through which the two cell-bodies enjoy protoplasmic communication. This type of organization is found in all the higher green plants. In the third type (Coenocytic) the nucleus alone divides, and the final result is a *coenocyte*—a single overgrown cell with a single cell-wall and many nuclei. This plan has been adopted by the Siphoneae (p. 89).

It is obvious that the first method is the most primitive and will be most generally practised by unicellular organisms; but whereas it has been abandoned by the higher plants, it seems to have been retained by the higher animals. Almost the only difference between the division of a protozoan and a metazoan cell lies in the fact that the two daughter-cells separate in the one case, cohere in the other. The essential separateness of the cohering cells is well seen in the collar-cells of simple Calcareous Sponges like Clathrina; here indeed there is even no continuity of coherence during normal life (p. 93).

Similar if less strikingly separate cells can be seen in many other groups of multicellular animals, and there can be very little doubt that the first method of division was employed by the common ancestor of all Metazoa[1]; true party-walls like those of filamentous plants do not exist in animals, and animal syncytia (tissues formed by the coenocytic method) are undoubtedly secondary.

We must now try and see what these facts mean. In the filamentous type the units are still homologous, as units, with the original units we called cells (p. 56); but they have sacrificed a considerable amount of independence. The whole mode of division by which they arise is an obvious adaptation to a state of existence where each is to be part of a continuous whole.

[1] It is more than probable that Sponges have an ancestry quite separate from the rest of the Metazoa: if so, then the common ancestor of Sponges employed, though quite independently, the same method as the ancestor of the Metazoa proper.

In Metazoa the separation of the cells is as a rule total, and if protoplasmic continuity exists, it appears to be secondarily produced. As regards their mode of cell-division, therefore, the Metazoa are more primitive than the Metaphyta; yet in spite of—or perhaps because of—this very separateness of their units, there has been a much greater division of labour between different kinds of units in animals than in plants.

To sum up: the cells of the higher plants and of the higher animals are both true cells—they are both broadly homologous with the original units of living matter. But the mode of cell-division in the two groups, in so far as it concerns the separation of the cells and the formation of the boundary between them, is *not* homologous.

INDEX

f = figure.   *n* = note.